# Get Rich in Small Business

## The 1980 Classic
## Secret Operating Manual

## 1999 UPDATE:

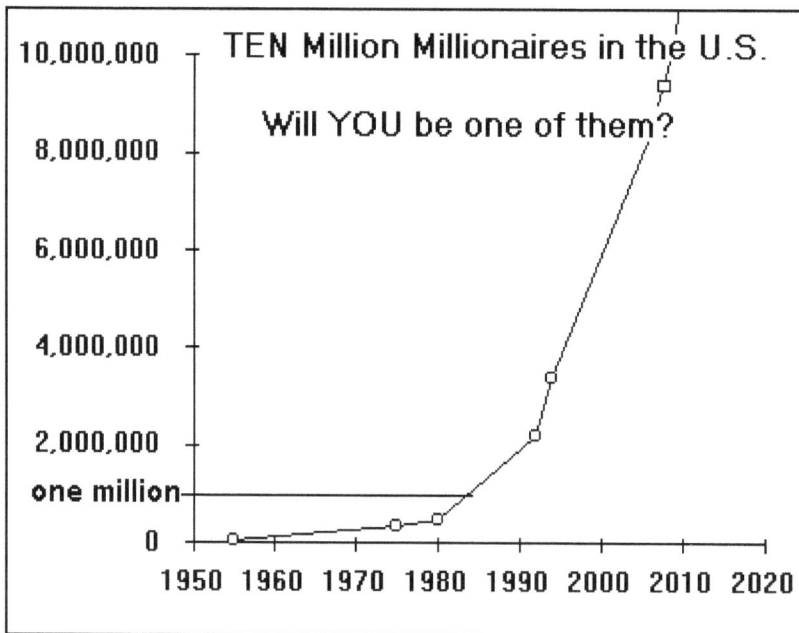

TEN Million Millionaires in the U.S.

Will YOU be one of them?

10,000,000
8,000,000
6,000,000
4,000,000
2,000,000
one million
0

1950 1960 1970 1980 1990 2000 2010 2020

## In 1980 Edition:

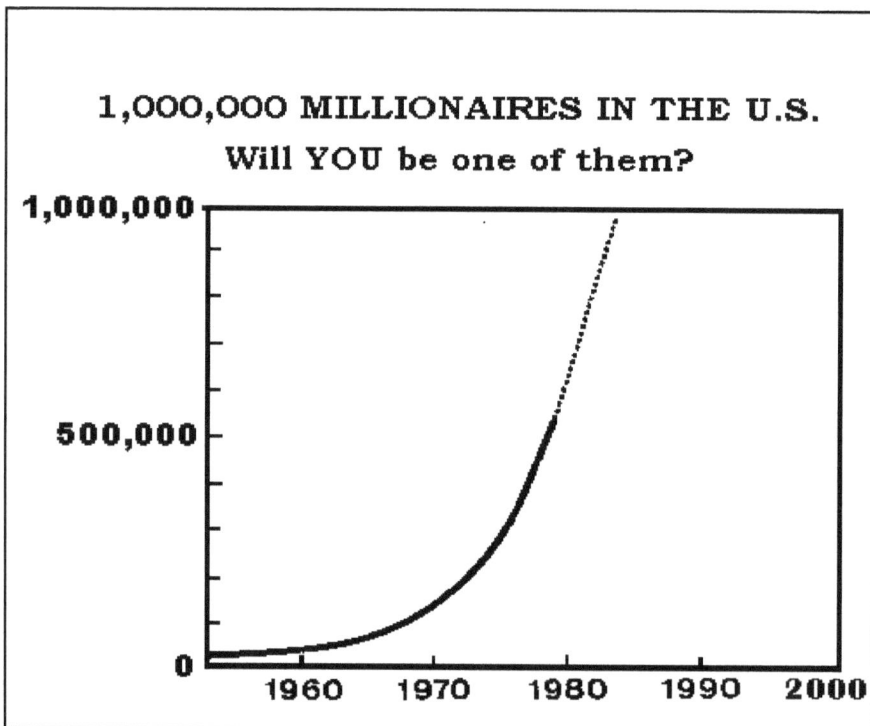

1,000,000 MILLIONAIRES IN THE U.S.

Will YOU be one of them?

1,000,000

500,000

0

1960 1970 1980 1990 2000

# Get Rich in Small Business

## The Small-Business Secret Operating Manual

First Edition 1980
Notes added 1999 and 2015

Mason A. Clark

Frontal Lobe ®
Los Altos, California

Library of Congress Control Number: 2015906457

ISBN:    978-0-931400-08-7

Printed in the United States of America

GetRich-037.wpd
Website -- possibly updates at:  http://frontal-lobe.info

Frontal Lobe ®
Los Altos, California

## Preface

This is a book about FREE ENTERPRISE. Some readers will call it a book about CAPITALISM.

### Where is the source of the wealth that makes the owners of some small businesses very rich?

The FREE ENTERPRISE system is the most effective system yet devised for producing goods and services the people need and want. If you know its secret you can make the system work better for the benefit of all of us.

YOU CAN BECOME A MILLIONAIRE by using the system--if you know the Secret Source of wealth and the method of using that source. Anyone can learn. Tens of thousands of people become millionaires in America every year.

# Seven Possibilities

There are seven possible sources of wealth in business--the contacts between the company and the world. Listed here are the people who bring money to the company and those who take money away from the company:

*1- the banker (if there is one)*

*2- the buyer of your company (if any)*

*3- the owner*

*4- customers*

*5- suppliers*

*6- employees*

*7- the government*

# Table of Contents

# 1 - The Source of Your Wealth

## Who has the wealth NOW?

Owner and employees work together in the company. You have taken some risk in starting the company (in a later chapter you will learn how to make the risk negligible). You must make the crucial decisions. You may be the smartest person in your company or you may not be. You may be the hardest worker in your company or you may not be. But you deserve to get rich in return for creating jobs. The system is set up to give you great wealth as a reward for your contribution to our economy and society.

However, no matter how smart you are and no matter how hard you work, there are only seven days in a week and twenty-four hours in a day. You can only do so much. Some two or three of your employees, taken together, are doing as much as you are. Perhaps one is a manager who can take your place when you sell out. But they probably are not going to get rich but they are the source of the wealth of a business owner.

Owners rarely talk about their wealth and rarely write books about it. When they do so it is to brag of their wisdom, not to reveal where their money came from. Accountants find it difficult to show the facts on the financial statements and hesitate to even try to do so.

There are exceptions. A San Francisco attorney, Louis Kelso, has written a book: <u>How to Turn Eighty Billion Workers into Capitalists on Borrowed Money</u>. He urges companies to adopt employee stock-ownership plans, commonly called "Kelso" plans or "ESOP's." Such plans would give employees a share in the company and presumably a share of the wealth.


1999 NOTE: That book is probably out of print. Amazon now (Aug.1999) shows a new book (which I haven't read): Democracy and Economic Power : Extending the Esop Revolution Through Binary Economics by Louis O. Kelso, and Patricia H. Kelso

Employers are secretive about the wages paid to employees. When I was a Vice-President of a West-coast electronic company, I often set the wages of employees. On my request, the Manager of our personnel department would take out of a locked lower desk drawer a secret book. It was a tabulation of the wages paid by all of the nearby electronic companies for each category of worker. This information was collected among the companies by their industry association. It was distributed so that each company would know how much to pay and wouldn't compete for employees by paying higher wages. The existence of the book was a tightly-kept secret.

For employees to be a continuing source of wealth, they must not find out how the wealth is divided. Employees are generally content. Most workers are not even organized. Strikes usually involve minor working condition disputes and requests for small wage increases. The wage increases are only partially proportioned to increases in productivity and don't quite keep up with inflation. The increases do not touch the employee / owner sharing of the wealth. The employees have at most a vague feeling that something may be wrong with their share of the wealth they create.

You, as the owner of a small company, will not increase your employee's awareness of the situation by flaunting your wealth--at least not in your home town. You will spend it quietly at one of your homes and freely on trips and private clubs.

After reading this book, you will know the importance of your employees, you will treat them better than will owners who have not learned the truth. You will build your company more wisely. That is to say; you will get richer quicker.

You may not yet believe that employees are the source of wealth. It is a fact not readily accepted by the owners of companies. Let us look at the other possible five sources. Then in the next chapters you will see the details of how employees are the source and how that can be shown in financial statements.

## Six Who'll Never Make You Rich

Let's examiner the six groups of people who carry money to and from your company but won't make you wealthy.

1. Your banker, if you have one, will insist on taking out more money than he puts in. Bankers will not be the source of anyone's wealth. Bankers make loans. They demand the return of the money--with interest. A loan may be helpful but by itself it only takes money out.

When you get a loan, your assets increase but your liabilities increase even more. Your net worth goes down. The drop in your net worth is caused by the additional liability for the interest on the loan. By borrowing, you decrease your wealth.

2. The buyer of your company (if there ever is one) expects the company to be a source of wealth for him. He wasn't in sight while your company was growing and you were living like a millionaire. The buyer, if there ever is one, cannot be the source of your wealth. He merely converts into cash the wealth you already have.

3. You, the owner, are not the source of your own wealth--except in some ego-trip sense. But there may be other owners, shareholders perhaps, or partners. All of these part owners will expect--and demand--to take wealth out of the company when you do. Owners take wealth out, not put it in. (They labor they put in is wealth, but how much can anyone do in a week that has only seven days of 24 hours each?)

4. Customers may seem to be the source of wealth. They pay your company money, but they take out products or services. They are careful to take out as much as they put in. If they can buy your product cheaper elsewhere, they will. The customers may be other companies who are getting rich too. It is a principle of free trade that each party benefits by the trade. Customers take out as much as they put in. If you try to get more out of them than you give them you'll only help your competitors take away your business. In a later chapter you will learn the facts about profit: that it may be best to not make a profit.

5. The suppliers of material bring value to your company in the form of goods you need in the conduct of your business. In return, they take out money. Like your customers, they will go elsewhere if the deal is not fair. Like you, the suppliers are companies that are making them rich. They cannot be the source of wealth.

Some company owners do not understand that the customers and suppliers are not the source of their wealth. They try to cheat the customers and suppliers by making unfair trades of money and goods. They charge the customers "all the trade will bear" and a little more. They demand lower prices from suppliers until the suppliers go out of business or refuse to sell to them. Suppliers who are not fairly treated have ways of getting even.

*A friend of mine with a million dollar company noticed that one of his customers had a habit of being unreasonably slow to pay for the machines he purchased. He walked into the customer's factory "to adjust the machine" he had sold to them--but not yet paid for. Then he announced that he would have to take the machine back to the factory for repairs, walked out with it, and refused to sell them anything without cash payment in advance. They will never get special services from his company.*

If you don't treat your suppliers fairly--let them get rich too--they will serve you poorly. You won't get rich with unhappy suppliers. Your good suppliers will help you get rich so they can get rich too. There must be, somewhere else, a source of wealth for both of you.

6. Finally, the government. The government exists to provide certain critical services including national defense, police, courts, and the national infrastructure of roads, libraries, schools, bridges, prisons, water lines, sewer lines and much else. Without such facilities and services it would be impossible to operate your business. You pay taxes for them and, by-and-large, you get what you pay for. If not, you have the vote and, when you're wealthy you can make some campaign contributions. Essential as it is, the government makes it possible for you to become wealthy but is not the source of the wealth.

We have eliminated six of the seven six possibilities: customers, suppliers, bankers, yourself, the buyer of your company (if any), and the government. None of them will make you rich but they'll help. There can be only one source: your employees.

At this point, some readers will still not believe that employees are the source of wealth. There is a good reason for your doubt. Your doubt is caused by your deeply set beliefs.

Anyone who has an interest in going into business and anyone who is already in business believes that free enterprise, capitalism, and the American way are good. They are absolutely right. A nation in which people can go into business for themselves will produce more goods and services for the people and provide more and better jobs than any other system. The free system is good but it is too easy to slip from knowing it is good to thinking that the system is exploiting the workers. It is fear of such thinking that keeps us from openly recognizing the role of workers in creating the wealth of business owners. We fear getting on the slippery slope from fact to fiction, but it is helpful to know the facts.

In the following chapters you will see how the system works and how employees are the source of wealth. You will see financial statements that show the dollars that employees give you to make your company grow and to make you wealthy.

Before looking at the details of the source of wealth, you should know where the wealth is. Employees have only a portion of the wealth. They only create it. They have been doing so in the United States for more than 200 years. Let's learn who now has the vast wealth that employees have generated.

The wealth distribution in the United States is important to small-business owner for two reasons: You need to know where the money is to know who can buy your product. Secondly, if you know how wealthy are the richest people, and how much of the nation's money they possess, you will be inspired to get your share.

## Who Has the Wealth?

1999 NOTE: I have chosen to leave this section as it was written in 1980. The quantity of wealth has greatly increased and the distribution is more skewed. The total debt has exploded since 1980 as has the total wealth of the wealthiest.

The total personal wealth of the people of the United States amounts to about $6,000 billion, that is to say:  $6,000,000,000,000, One-fifth of that wealth is held by only one percent of the people. The wealth of the United States is owned by a small percentage of the people.

One-sixth of the wealth is held by only one-fourth of one percent of the people. These 548,000 members of the wealthy families have an average of $1,825,000 for each person, which is about six million dollars per family.

The illustration of the wealth distribution shows the ten equal groups of the population. Each of these groups has one-tenth of the people. There are 22 million persons in each group. You can see that the poorer half of the population share among them less than three-percent of the nation's wealth.

The richest 7% of the population has half of the nation's wealth.

The poorest half of the population has only 3% of the wealth.

The super-rich one-fourth of one percent have 16% of the wealth.

There are 520,000 millionaires United States in 1979.

The number of millionaires is growing by 15% each year. In 1985 there will be 180,400 new millionaires in that one year. Will you be one of them?

The number of millionaires is increasing much faster than the population and much faster than can be explained by inflation. The number of millionaires has been increasing at almost the same rate during years of little inflation.  Becoming a millionaire is one of the best ways for you to protect yourself from inflation.

The fact that 520,000 people are millionaires should incite you to get your share. The system is set up to encourage a few smart people to become very wealthy, leaving many to be poor or middle class. You surely want to be rich, not among the poor, and why be mediocre?

---

2015 Note added during editing:

As a matter of interest – and because this space is open –

1) The 85 richest people in the world have as much wealth as the 3.5 billion poorest.

2) Almost half of the world's wealth is now owned by just one percent of the population.

3) The wealth of the one percent richest people in the world amounts to $110 trillion. That's 65 times the total wealth of the bottom half of the world's population.

4) The richest one percent increased their share of income in 24 out of 26 countries for which we have data between 1980 and 2012.

5) In the US, the wealthiest one percent captured 95 percent of post-financial crisis growth since 2009, while the bottom 90 percent became poorer.

http://marginalrevolution.com/marginalrevolution/2014/12/sentences-about-wealth-inequality.html#sthash.RaobP9s6.dpuf

http://www.forbes.com/sites/laurashin/2014/01/23/the-85-richest-people-in-the-world-have-as-much-wealth-as-the-3-5-billion-poorest/

https://www.oxfam.org/en/research/working-few

# Who Has the Wealth?

1999 NOTE:  This was for 1980.

Each of these blocks of wealth
is owned by one-tenth of the
people of the United States.

The richest 10% of the people could
pay off all of our debts. They would
then still be the wealthiest group.

There are no debts.
There is only a distribution
of the wealth.

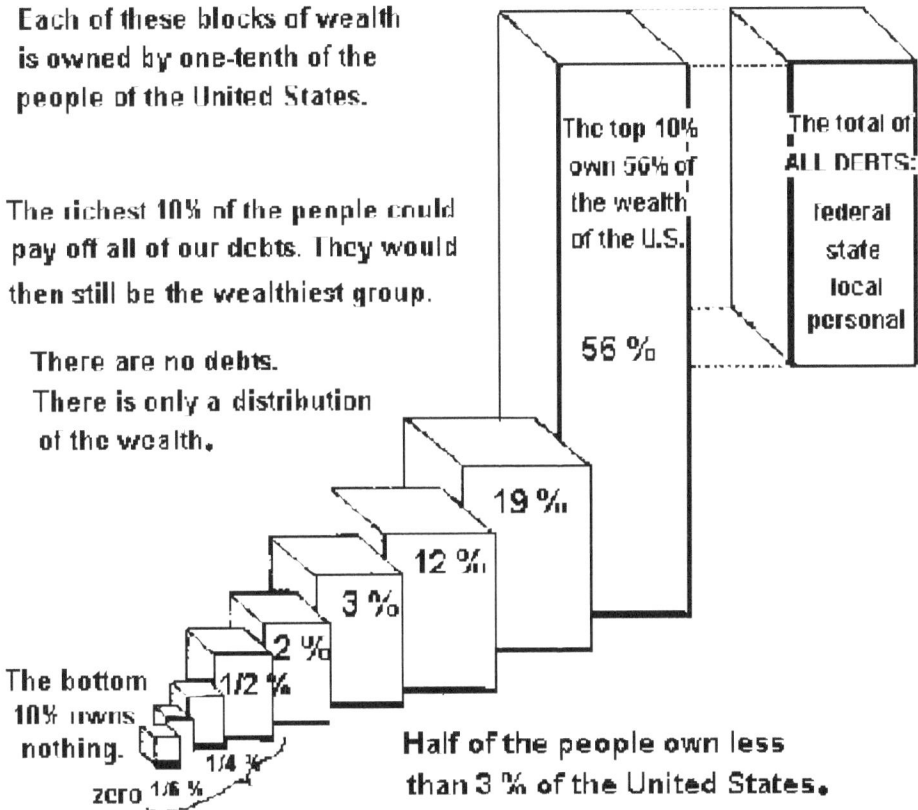

The top 10%
own 56% of
the wealth
of the U.S.

56 %

The total of
ALL DEBTS:
federal
state
local
personal

19 %

12 %

3 %

2 %

The bottom
10% owns
nothing.

1/2 %

1/4 %

zero 1/6 %

Half of the people own less
than 3 % of the United States.

## There are no debts

The richest ten percent of the people have more than half of the nation's wealth. They have more than $3,360,000,000,000.

The total of all government and personal debts in the United States, including the federal debt, all state debts, all city debts, all personal debts including home mortgages and installment buying, and all small business debts, but not the debts of corporations, is $2,940,000,000,000. The top ten percent of the wealthy could pay off all of those debts and still keep their positions as the richest of us all.

## There is only a distribution of the wealth

Go with the system. Become one of the chosen wealthy. Knowledge of the system of wealth has enabled many small-business owners to become wealthy rapidly. They found products or services they could sell at high prices to the wealthy people, examples are the famous-name luxury department stores, such as Nieman-Marcus, who cater to the rich.

The 520,000 millionaires are not smarter than you. A few had rich grandfathers who owned small business that grew. A few were lucky in real estate. Most of them stumbled on the secret source of wealth. They formed small companies to make a living and were surprised to find themselves rich.

Remember these facts and use them:

Half of the people have 97% of the wealth.
Half of the people have 3% of the wealth.

In which group will you be? To which group can you best sell your products or your services?

You need have only a small company to be a millionaire. Don't let the thought of owning such a large company scare you. You'll grow into it. Those millionaires are no smarter than you. If they can do it, so can you.

They once had to learn to tie their shoes, deal with accountants, choose good lawyers, and hire employees. In this book you will learn much of what you really need to know. You can fill in the details as they are needed for your particular business.

First, you must know exactly what it is you are going to do. You must have a target. Aristotle said it 2000 years ago: "Are you not more likely to score if you have a target?" In the next chapter you will see the accounting sheets needed for this target.

## Action

1. If you can't believe the number of millionaires and the way the wealth is distributed, ask your local librarian for the latest edition of the Statistical Abstracts of the United States and other sources of such information. Believe it. It can make you rich.

2. If you can't believe that your employees are the Secret Source of wealth, read on. You will believe it when you read the next chapters. Then you can use the information to make yourself wealthy.

# 2 - Your Little $1,000,000 Company

## Financial Statements Hide Things

> Note added in 2006: You should aim higher! One million dollars in 1980, when this book was first published, has become closer to ten million dollars and making it has become easier.

We must look for the Secret Source of wealth in the financial statements of companies, especially your company.

Knowing the source will lead us immediately to a method of making your company grow. The growth of your company gives you a hidden income-especially hidden from the income tax collector, but also hidden from all too many company owners who don't understand the system.

This is not a book on conventional accounting. In fact, such accounting is full of deceptions. No matter how much you think you know about accounting, don't skip this or the following chapter.

In order to understand the American Millionaire's Method of getting rich and the Secret Source of the millionaire's wealth, we must rearrange the financial statements so that they report reality, not fictions for the Internal Revenue Service and hot profit-hiding schemes to keep employees and the public happy. You, the company owner, must have a clear picture of what is really going on in your company.

You must learn about things that accountants do not write or talk about. In fact, the millionaires themselves will be annoyed with this exposure of their method by the revised financial statements in the next chapter. Some will say it isn't so. You be the judge.

What you need to know is: what size and sort of company do you need in order to be a millionaire? You must know a little about company financial statements and the numbers needed on your statements to make you a millionaire. In short, you need a target.

## The Growth of Net Worth is Income for You

Suppose your company is worth only $500,000 but is growing by 10% per year and pays you a salary of $30,000 after taxes. The yearly growth in value is $50,000. Added to your salary this gives you $80,000 income. It's not all ready cash. The $50,000 is <u>savings</u> just as if you had it in the bank, but growing faster.

There is an additional source of income. The government will give you, the company owner, many tax advantages which amount to additional income.

You can see that there is more than one way to be a millionaire. Straight salary is the most difficult. Growing net worth is easier. Let's set up your target company and learn what is happening.

If you have not been looking at company financial statements, don't worry, they are simple. Start by making out your own personal financial statements. During the time you own your company without incorporation, you will have to combine your personal affairs with the company when you make out your income-tax reports. For all other purposes you should keep separate statements. For our purpose here, we will concentrate on your company, but start with your personal statement as an introduction.

## Your Personal Balance Sheet – Now

You have a net worth equal to what you've got minus what you owe.

Net Worth = Assets - Liabilities     This way it is obvious

That's the basic equation of accounting. You could go to a business school and learn that in less than three months.  But they teach writing this way:

Assets = Liabilities + Net Worth

This equation always bothered me. It looks as though more Liabilities give you more Assets. Wrong idea of cause and effect. The equation either way is not about cause and effect. It is about balance on the Balance Sheet.

| The Basic Equation of Accounting | | | | |
|---|---|---|---|---|
| Assets | $ 5,000 | OR | Liabilities | $ 2,000 |
| -Liabilities | - $ 2,000 | | +Net Worth | $ 3,000 |
| | | | | |
| =Net Worth | $ 3,000 | | =Assets | $ 5,000 |

If book-keeping and accounting really worry you, get a copy of the book: Small Time Operator by Bernard Kamoroff, C.P.A. Written for the "little" man or women in business, especially in a small retail store. A pleasure to read, it is loaded with ideas about how to succeed with a small business, has many comments from small business experience, and gives additional references and forms for small-company book-keeping. Like all other books before this one you're reading, it does not mention the source of wealth.

1999 NOTE: This book by Kamoroff, recommended here in 1980, is now in its sixth edition and is listed by Amazon. I haven't seen this editon but it must be popular.

The source of wealth must be hidden somewhere in the book-keeping and in the financial statements. We'll find it.

You should have no trouble listing your assets and liabilities and subtracting to find your net worth. But you cannot do this precisely. The fact is that the best corporate financial statements are not accurate. It is necessary to make up arbitrary rules. Accountants have devised many such rules and some are more confusing than helpful.

It is not easy to determine what an asset is worth. For example, you own some old furniture. To find out what it's worth, you would have to get a dealer to come and look at it, then to be sure, you would have to get a second appraisal--and a third when the first two disagree. That gives you an estimate of the market value. But you aren't going to sell it so the real question is; what is it worth to you or what would it cost to replace?

Companies have old furniture, old machinery, old buildings, and old land. They don't know what they are worth, so the accountants have evolved and invented schemes called "generally accepted accounting principles applied on a consistent basis."

Property that wears out or gets old is "depreciated." By formulas that the Internal Revenuers approve, the initial cost is taken as the value, then reduced in an arbitrary way each year. Both the Assets and the Net Worth are reduced so the Balance Sheet still balances. The depreciation is listed among the costs on your Earnings, Income, or Profit and Loss Statement--as it's variously called--and thereby reduces both your profit and your income tax. Reducing profit is good. Reducing tax is good.

# YOUR PERSONAL FINANCIAL STATEMENT
## BALANCE SHEET (fill it out now)

**ASSETS**

Cash on hand and in bank          $_____

Savings accounts in banks         $_____

U.S. government bonds             $_____

Accounts and notes receivable     $_____

Life insurance cash value         $_____

Other stocks and bonds            $_____

Real estate                       $_____

Automobiles                       $_____

Other personal property           $_____

Other assets                      $_____

**TOTAL ASSETS** . . . . . . . . . . . . . . . . $_____

**LIABILITIES**

Accounts payable                  $_____

Notes payable to banks            $_____

Notes payable to others           $_____

Installment account (auto)        $_____

Installment account (_____)    $_____

Loans on life insurance           $_____

Mortgages on real estate          $_____

Unpaid taxes                      $_____

Other liabilities                 $_____

**TOTAL LIABILITIES** . . . . . . . . . . .$_____

**NET WORTH = ASSETS - LIABILITIES** . . . . . . $_____

There are trick formulas for depreciating fast or slow so to reduce the income tax. The simplest formula is to take a thing that will last five years and reduce its value by one-fifth each year. When you start making a lot of money, your accountant will use the tricks. You can wind up with equipment and perhaps a building which is written off your book but is still useable. Financial statements are full of such lies.

A different problem is posed by things that don't depreciate fast enough to get them off your books. For example, land. Land usually increases in dollar value. Accountants don't like to acknowledge this. Their rule is: if there is no transaction, there is no change in the value on the books. So, many companies have hidden assets. They have assets whose value has increased far beyond their value on the books.

I was once robbed by this rule. I owned a piece of a company that had bought land in a fast-developing city. The land went up greatly in market value. When the company forcefully bought back my shares, they ignored the value of the land in determining the price of the shares. The accountants will have their way.

Now you know all you need to know to make up a balance sheet that will satisfy the accountants and the banks and the Internal Revenue Service. As your company grows, your bookkeepers and accountants and tax lawyer will take care of the complex details.

Make up a balance sheet for your personal property. Do it, it's a fun exercise and useful. Figure the depreciation and market or replacement values in any way that seems reasonable to you. No one is looking over your shoulder. Later, if you want to expand your company rapidly by borrowing, you will need just such a balance sheet to show the bank. In a later chapter, you will learn how to expand safely and rapidly with little or no borrowing.

You can use the balance-sheet form provided here. You may not have many of the items listed--you don't have the million yet. You can make a sheet just as accurate as any an accountant can prepare for you. He can only put down what you tell him.

It will be nice if your assets are more than your liabilities. They may not be. Ten percent of the people have assets less than their liabilities. They have a negative net worth. They expect to pay their debts, mostly due to installment buying, from future earnings. Inflation will help them if it doesn't ruin us all.

> 1999 NOTE: I suspect that more people are in debt today because credit card debt has grown explosively since 1980. I've seen a projection of $660 billion of credit card debt in the year 2000

Even people with negative net worth can start companies--and often do. Not having money is one of the strongest incentives for getting rich.

## Your $1,000,000 Balance Sheet

The Balance Sheet for your company will depend upon factors which develop during the growth of the company and upon the nature of the business in which you choose to engage. The Value Line Investment Survey publishes the total balance sheet of 900 industrial, retail, and transportation companies. The $1,000,000 Balance Sheet shown here is based upon the ratios reported by Value Line. Your new company will differ from this, but the difference will be mostly in your favor. This is a conservative balance sheet for a small company. You can do better.

You will not have accumulated so much depreciation and you should have less of such liabilities as mortgages and loans. Your assets should be higher and your liabilities should be lower, if you follow the instruction in later chapters. Therefore your net worth will be greater.

The $1,000,000 Balance Sheet is based on annual sales of $285,000. This is calculated to allow you to live like a millionaire. After you study the Earnings Statement and learn the principle of using employees to make yourself a millionaire, you may wish to revise the Balance Sheet and the Earnings Statement to suit your own goals. (A retail store must have higher sales to make you a millionaire.) You may adjust your target to the level you think you need. Look at your target again after you have finished the book and understand the whole story.

At this point, some readers will feel that they are being cheated--that I am calling them "millionaires" when they have a company and an income too small.

It is a common illusion that millionaires are mysterious tycoons surrounded with bodyguards and tax lawyers. We read about Howard Hughes [and Bill Gates--1999 editing] and don't notice the owner of the little factory on a back street. He is not eccentric, doesn't show off his wealth, looks human, and has more money than he knows how to spend.

*In the beautiful village on the Wisconsin River where I came from and in the town where I now live, and in your town, there are printing shops. The owner of the Wisconsin village shop writes, sets type, prints, and mails the town paper. He prints nothing else. The California shop prints everything except newspapers. Neither has employees. When I asked each owner why he didn't have employees to help him do more, they both replied that "employees were too much trouble." Each business owner is making a bare living.*

*Also in my California town, and up the Wisconsin river a few miles, are printing shops with a different way of doing business.*

*When George Woodman decided to get out of the electronic industry, he studied the small printing-shop business. He chose to start with used equipment and used employees--both had experience and cost little. He knew the value of employees in creating wealth. In a few years he developed a printing business with 12 employees.*

*You know that these employees are the source of wealth and you will learn in the next chapter how much 12 employees are worth to the owner of the company. George Woodman is rapidly becoming a wealthy man.*

The company owner's income is much greater than it seems, and the government provides the company owner with tax advantages which add still more to his income. In this chapter you learn about true owner income. In a later chapter you will learn about the government's contributions.

First--the Balance Sheet. Look at the model sheet. It has assets divided into Current Assets and Plant and Equipment. The Current Assets are moneys you can get your hand on quickly. The Accounts Receivable may have a few bad debts. Make allowance for them. The Inventories are supposed to be saleable at the value you have placed on them. The sale may never take place at that price. Inventory lies are commonplace.

---

1999 NOTE: I'm reminded of the company that I knew well as a competitor. When the auditors were expected they hastily hid their inventory in the basement. They were hiding profits from the IRS, were never caught, but eventually were overrun by history. Don't ask.

---

Accountants assume that you are not actually going to suddenly liquidate your company. They assume that you have a "going concern" and that the inventory will be sold in due time.

# YOUR $1,000,000 COMPANY BALANCE SHEET

| ASSETS | % of sales | Based on sales of $ 285,000 |
|---|---|---|
| CURRENT ASSETS | | |
| Cash and equivalents | 6 % | $17,000 |
| Accounts receivable | 13% | 37,000 |
| Inventories | 14% | 40,000 |
| Other current assets | | 6,000 |
| PLANT and EQUIPMENT | | |
| Plant and equipment | 53% | 150,000 |
| Less depreciation | 23% | 65,000 |
| Other assets | 2% | 25,000 |
| TOTAL ASSETS | | $ 210,000 |
| LIABILITIES | | |
| CURRENT LIABILITIES | | |
| Notes payable | 9% | 26,000 |
| Accounts payable | 10% | 29,000 |
| LONG-TERM DEBT | | |
| Mortgage | 18% | 52,000 |
| Long-term loans | 2% | 5,000 |
| TOTAL LIABILITIES | | $ 112,000 |
| NET WORTH | | |
| Owner's investment | 0.35% | 1,000 |
| Retained earnings | 34% | 97,000 |
| TOTAL NET WORTH | 34% | $ 98,000 |
| LIABILITIES & NET WORTH | | $ 210,000 |

The Plant and Equipment, less depreciation, have value but the money is not readily available. You can't use them to pay off your current debts. Your Current Liabilities will have to be paid by your Current Assets. Of course, this isn't to be done all at once. There is a flow, day-by-day, of assets paying off liabilities. Most businessmen think the Current Assets should be about twice the Current Liabilities to be safe. This means you have some extra current assets to use in the operation of the business. These "spare" currents assets are called "working capital." When you don't have working capital you are in trouble.

Your Liabilities are divided into Current and Long-term Debt. On any day you will owe something to your suppliers. This is your Accounts Payable. Presumably you're going to pay them. You are also going to pay your current notes that come due. Some of the Notes Payable are payments on loans that are actually long-term. A mortgage is the common example of a long-term liability which has current liability payment requirements.

When you subtract the Liabilities from the Assets you get your Net Worth. To explain where the Net Worth came from, it is customary to list the investment by the owner or owners and, in addition--and hopefully much larger--the money earned and kept in the company. These Retained Earnings exist only on paper, as an explanation of the Net Worth. They are not sitting in a bank account. Everything in Net Worth could be regarded as a loan from the owner to the company.

The Net Worth is also called the "book value" of the company. But the book value of a company is not what the company is worth. In fact, the Net Worth is best regarded as a book-keeping tool and little else. Companies are commonly sold for much more or for much less than their Net Worth. Having a company with a Net Worth of $1,000,000 may not make you a millionaire. It could be a bankrupt company or it could be worth much more than a million dollars.

To learn the true value of your company, we must look at the Earnings Statement. This used to be called a "Profit and Loss Statement," but "profit" became a dirty word and "loss" always was. Since "earning money" is considered "good," the P and L Statement is now called the "Earnings Statement" and everybody's happy. Companies no longer brag of making a profit. In fact, their reported profit is quaintly small. The reason for this and the truth about profits you will learn in the next chapter.

1999 NOTE: It has been observed that corporation profits have been falling steadily in recent decades. The reason for this is better management, including the use of computers to provide up-to-date accounting reports to management. Low profits are good (less taxes).

## Your $1,000,000 Earnings Statement

The Earnings Statement always starts at the top with the "Gross Income" or "Sales." On your personal earnings statement this will be a salary or wage and perhaps interest on savings accounts and other income. Here "income" is what comes in, not what you pay income tax on. It is the amount paid to you for services, for the use of your money, for the use of a rental house you own, as a gift, or for whatever reason you receive money.

The second item on the Earnings Statement is the "Cost." This is usually itemized, at least in a few large groups. Your company will have Labor, Material, Overhead, Interest, and Growth Expenses. Overhead includes rent and utilities and management and other items which cannot be easily related to a specific product going out the door. The Earnings Statements for large corporations usually do not list labor and material separately. This is because they have many products with differing labor/material relationships, and because the stockholders don't much care about these numbers.

The Earning Statement for the million-dollar company will be shown here in two ways. The first Earnings Statement shown is conventional except that the reinvestment for growth is listed separately and again at the bottom of the statement along with the owner's total income.

In the next chapter, the Earnings Statement will be revised so as to reveal certain facts obscured by the conventional statement. It is necessary to first understand the conventional statement.

The second item on the Earnings Statement is the "Cost." This is usually itemized, at least in a few large groups. Your company will have Labor, Material, Overhead, Interest, and Growth Expenses. Overhead includes rent and utilities and management and other items which cannot be easily related to a specific product going out the door. The Earnings Statements for large corporations usually do not list labor and material separately. This is because they have many products with differing labor/material relationships, and because the stockholders don't much care about these numbers.

The Earning Statement for the million-dollar company will be shown here in two ways. The first Earnings Statement shown is conventional except that the reinvestment for growth is listed separately and again at the bottom of the statement along with the owner's total income.

In the next chapter, the Earnings Statement will be revised so as to reveal certain facts obscured by the conventional statement. It is necessary to first understand the conventional statement.

## YOUR $1,000,000 COMPANY

CONVENTIONAL EARNINGS STATEMENT
---with the wealth source concealed---
-----with tax-collection obscured-----

| | | |
|---|---|---|
| SALES | | $285,000 |
| COSTS | | |
| Labor | 64,000 | |
| Material | 78,000 | |
| Overhead | 37,000 | |
| Interest on Loans | 6,000 | |
| Growth Expenses | 51,000 | 239,000 |
| REPORTED PRE-TAX INCOME | | 46,000 |
| INCOME TAX | | 17,000 |
| OWNER-REPORTED AFTER-TAX INCOME | | $29,000 |

-------------------------------------------------------

*GROWTH OF VALUE OF THE COMPANY  $51,000

*OWNER'S TOTAL AFTER-TAX INCOME   $80,000

*OWNER'S EQUIVALENT NET-ASSETS   $1,000,000

* usually omitted from conventional Earnings Statements

You can prepare a personal Earnings Statement. You do this, in effect, when you prepare a Form 1040 income-tax return. The income-tax return distorts the Earnings Statement according to the whims of the Congress and the IRS. What you want is to list your money coming in, subtract the money you spent in order to make that money come in, and subtract all other expenses until you have left your savings, if any. In effect, your savings are your "profit" or what companies now call their "earnings." You could enjoy life with no profit whatsoever but a loss can cause trouble so it's better to stay on the profit side. New companies with big money commonly operate without a profit for a long time.

The statement shown here is unconventional in one important respect. Those expenses which are not needed for the production and sale of the present products are listed separately as Growth Expenses. Companies do list their Research and Development expenses separately, but these are only a part of the total expenditure intended to provide growth. In addition, money is spent on new-product engineering, cost-reduction beyond what is necessary to meet competition, and new plants and equipment not immediately needed. All of these expenses reduce profits and taxes. All add to the net worth of the company owner.

The source of the cash to invest in growth expenses is the gross profit you make on sales. You may also borrow money or invest more of your own money. The profit reinvested results in an increase in Net Worth on the Balance Sheet. The Net Worth increase does not show on the conventional Earnings Statement or on the owner's income tax forms. Nevertheless, the increase in Net Worth is an increase in the owner's wealth. It is income for the owner. Our Earnings Statement therefore calls attention to this income on the bottom lines.

You may wonder why no salary is shown for the owner. This is a convention required by the income-tax laws. There is only one income to be taxed, not an owner salary and a separate company profit. If the company is incorporated, this changes. A corporation has a life of its own--and its own income-tax. But because good management of the corporation will reduce its profits and income tax to a minimum, the IRS will insist that the owner/manager be paid a customary salary so that his income tax can be collected in addition to the tax on the corporation profit.

To know how well your company is doing, you should include on your Earnings Statement a salary such as you would need to pay to a hired manager. We will do this in the next chapter, along with our other revisions to make the Statement realistic, and to reveal the millionaire's source of wealth.

But, before going on, you should study the Earnings Statement carefully. If you feel that the company is not big enough for you, wait until you finish this book, then pencil in your changes. What is most essential is that you understand that THE GROWTH OF THE COMPANY CONSTITUTES INCOME FOR YOU .

Company value is a savings account, but not so endangered by inflation. In a later chapter you will learn how inflation will steal your bank savings account. Inflation will not affect your company value. All of the figures on the Statements will go up with inflation, including your wealth. Your wealth can go up without limit--faster than inflation.

Most readers are surprised to learn that one can be a millionaire by owning so small a company. The fact is that the company growth is a continuous, hidden income nowhere shown on the conventional books. This hidden income continually increasing the net worth of the owner is the millionaire's method.

The $1,000,000 financial statements here describe a profitable and efficient small company. Nevertheless, the ratios among the figures are typical of large companies. A small company with you as a competent manager should do better. You don't have to be ashamed of starting small. Here are the Earnings Statement numbers for two years of a company that started small.

# Hewlett-Packard

### THE RESULT FROM A SMALL START

|                            | First Year  | 1978            |
|----------------------------|-------------|-----------------|
| SALES                      | $ 5,368.64  | $ 2,361,000,000 |
| COSTS and EXPENSES         |             |                 |
| Cost of goods sold         | 2,666.38    | 1,106,000,000   |
| Research and Development   | 0.00        | 204,000,000     |
| Marketing                  | 410.12      | 362,000,000     |
| Administrative and General | 649.02      | 291,000,000     |
|                            | 3,725.52    | 1,963,000,000   |
| INCOME before taxes        | 1,643.12    | 398,000,000     |
| TAXES                      | 0.00        | 195,000,000     |
| NET INCOME                 | 1,652.89    | 203,000,000     |

1999 NOTE: Here follows the same little table revised for 1999. This is a demonstration of compounded growth: a few percent each year for year after year. The annual growth rate from 1978 to 1999 was 15%

# Hewlett-Packard

## THE RESULT FROM A SMALL START CONTINUES

|  | First Year | March 1999 |
|---|---|---|
| SALES | $ 5,368.6 | $ 47,064,000,000 |
| COSTS and EXPENSES |  |  |
| Cost of goods sold | 2,666.38 |  |
| Research and Development | 0.00 |  |
| Marketing | 410.12 |  |
| Administrative and Genera | 1,649.02 |  |
|  | 3,725.52 |  |
| INCOME before taxes | 1,643.12 | $ 4,091,000,000 |
| TAXES | 0.00 | 1,146,000,000 |
| NET INCOME | 1,652.89 | 2,945,000,000 |

You may be willing to settle for less success than Hewlett-Packard. But the principle is the same. A "small" company that will make you a millionaire is well within reach. As Dave Packard once told me: "IT'S EASY TO MAKE A MILLION DOLLARS. THE QUESTION IS: 'DO YOU WANT TO?'"

Some do not want to. Some want to but shouldn't. What Packard was suggesting was that doing what is necessary, then living with the results, is not the life for everyone. Most men are more content to let the bosses make the decisions, do the worrying, and have the wealth. The risk-taking is not by the owners but by the workers, living on their wages. You are reading this because you are not satisfied to risk your life to inflation, getting laid off, losing pensions, and the other hazards of being a worker. Owning a company is safer.

# 3 - The Millionaire's Secret Source

## Profits, Taxes, and Your Employees

Your source of wealth is not to be seen in the conventional accounting statements. It is not customers and it is not profits.

The profits of companies are small--a few percent. The growth of most companies exceeds their reported profits. A few companies grow rapidly and make their founders wealthy while operating at a loss--profit is not necessary. The profits reported on the bottom line certainly are not the source of wealth and not the source of company growth.

Where then does all the wealth come from? Somewhere in the system there is a source. We already know what it must be: employees. We must find where that source is concealed in the books. To do this, we must rewrite the financial statements.

Because of the tax laws, the accountants play all kinds of games with every item on the statements. This makes such statements obscure to the untrained reader. The goal is to pay as little in taxes as possible. This is proper and legal.

In the words of the distinguished Judge Learned Hand:

*"Any one may so arrange his affairs that his taxes shall be as low as possible. He is not bound to choose that pattern which will best pay the Treasury. There is not even a patriotic duty to increase one's taxes."*

There is good reason not to increase your company's taxes. The taxes each company pays must be added to the prices of its products and services.

Each company collects tax from its customers and mails that collection to the government. The tax must be kept as low as possible in order to keep prices low.

The company that lets its taxes rise may lose out in the marketplace. On the other hand, to make the company look good to investors or to a future buyer of the company, the company's income must be made to look high and growing.

A company needs to keep three sets of financial records and publish three sets of statements. One set would be for the income-tax collectors and would show a low income. One set would go the shareholders and show a high income and growth of income. The third set will tell the manager what is going on in the company. No dishonesty is implied. Each reader has a different need.

You need the manager's books and statements because only there will you see the re-investment of profits that are not reported on the conventional statements. And you need to know the truth about the collection of taxes.

Because you don't pay taxes--you only collect them--your only concern is with their affect on your prices. You do not need to worry about paying taxes. You do not pay them--you collect them. This cannot be said too often: companies do not pay taxes, they collect them. No company has a mysterious pocket from which it draws money to pay taxes. Companies collect taxes from customers for the Internal Revenue Service.

## The Source of Your Wealth

Nowhere in the conventional accounting statements is the source of wealth revealed. The Balance Sheet is silent. The Earnings Statement begins with Sales, as though that were the source. They are not, essential though they are. Customers take care of to receive from you products or services equal to the money they bring to you.

We must segregate those expenses that are necessary for the operation of the company from those that make the company grow. The source of wealth must be the source of growth money.

The costs we are looking for are those which are discretionary: The money the company does not have to spend to stay in business. The owner makes the decision to spend these discretionary moneys because he wants the company to grow. If he wished, he could take the money home. He is too wise to do that.

The expenses of research and development and engineering to create new products are obvious growth expenses. Advertising to give the company an image or to increase sales is a growth expense.

Cost reduction efforts to increase sales over competitors are growth expenses. On the other hand, some product development, cost reduction, and advertising are necessary just to keep the company in business at a steady level. Such expenses are not growth expenses but are necessary costs of staying in business.

The distinction between "necessary" and "growth" is therefore not always clear. Some company owners do not understand this distinction and do not attempt to make it. Their company either fails to grow because they do not make the growth effort, or their company gets into trouble by spending too much for growth and depleting the resources it needs to operate its business.

The identification of growth expenses will make it possible to make adjustments in your flow of money to adapt to business conditions. When business slows down (because of the economy, weather, strikes by suppliers, or for any other reason) you can cut back your growth expenses without endangering the continued operation of your company. In a later chapter you will learn how to make such adjustments easy for you to carry out.

Well-managed companies show a steady but small bottom-line profit year after year. They can do this because they can adjust their growth expenses so as to control the bottom lines of their Earnings Statements, while maintaining the regular operations of the company. Clever treasurers often make such adjustments from quarter to quarter, making bad quarters look good. Stockholders don't like to see bad quarters.

To keep your costs segregated between "necessary" and "growth," record your expenditures in separate accounts. Do not let your accountants do this sorting. You and your workers and supervisors must do this. Have a list of specific projects. Know which are necessary and which are for growth.

Many small businesses, especially little retail stores, do not keep accounts that segregate costs. That is one reason retail stores rarely make millionaires. Most retail store owners are doing only what they must to stay in business. If the owner of a retail store knew the difference between "necessary" and "growth" expenses, he could get more growth and more wealth.

---

1999 NOTE: You can be certain that Sam Walton knew the difference. He invested in growth and grew WalMart.

The discretionary money, generated by the work of your employees, is the source of wealth. It appears hardly at all on financial statements. If employees are so important, why do they not appear on the Earnings Statement? Most such statements do not list labor and material separately. They list only "Cost of Products Sold." And even if labor is shown separately, there is no indication that it is anything but a necessary cost--something to be reduced if possible. In fact, this cost should be <u>increased</u> if possible.

Employees generate a surplus which you can use for the growth expenses of your company or take home or plow back in your company as capital. We need an Earnings Statement that shows this. You will find such a statement here--and nowhere else.

## Your Factual Earnings Statement

The Factual Earnings Statement shown here can be prepared only after the conventional statement has been made. This is necessary because the Internal Revenue Service calculates your income tax on the basis of the conventional statements they require – distorted though they are --. After you have your conventional statement, and have calculated your income tax, you can prepare the factual statement.

Taxes are paid by the individual consumers, the residents of the nation. **There is no one else**. When you set the price of the products or services of your company, you must include something for the taxes the government wants you to collect. Because the government prefers that voters not be aware that they are paying taxes, the taxes are computed on the company income rather than on its sales. Therefore, to understand what is really going on, you must compute your income as though you were not collecting taxes. Then you compute your tax.

The tax is actually paid by your customers as a part of the price. The Factual Earnings Statement therefore shows the tax as a subtraction from your Gross Sales. The $17,000 is what you will collect from the customers and send to the government, leaving you with sales of $268,000.

To arrive at the $17,000 figure for your tax, it was necessary to compute in the manner shown on the conventional Earnings Statement. That statement is, in effect, simply a work-sheet used in the computation of your true statement.

The tax shown ($17,000) is intended to be representative and cannot be an actual calculation because I do not have your personal information: deductions, exclusions, family size, interest paid and collected, other income, and so forth. Because your company is owned exclusively by you--no partners, no incorporation--your income tax form will combine the company with your personal accounts.

After the subtraction of the tax you collected from your customers and sent to the government, you have Net Sales of $268,000. Your necessary costs are listed separately. One of your necessary costs is your own salary. You have to live. A salary for the manager is always a necessary cost and should be listed so as not to deceive yourself about your costs.

# Your $1,000,000 COMPANY
the Millionaire's Source revealed
<u>FACTUAL EARNINGS STATEMENT</u>

|  | | Worksheet | Finished Statement |
|---|---|---|---|
| GROSS SALES (less sales tax) | | $ 285,000 | 285,000 |
| INCOME TAX collected from customers | | | 17,000 |
| Net Sales of products or services | | | 268,000 |
| **NECESSARY COSTS** | | | |
| Owner's Salary | $ 20,000 | | |
| Labor | 64,000 | | |
| Materia | 1 78,000 | | |
| Overhead | 40,000 | | |
| Interest | 6,000 | 208,000 | 208,000 |
| COMPANY PROFIT (workers' surplus) | | 77,000 | 60,000 |
| **USES of WORKERS' SURPLUS** | | | |
| Reinvested for Growth | | 51,000 | 51,000 |
| Unused Profit | | 26,000 | 9,000 |
| OWNER's SALARY drawn | | 20,000 | 20,000 |
| **OWNER REPORTS:** | | | |
| OWNER'S  PRE-TAX INCOME | | 46,000 | |
| INCOME TAX | | 17,000 | |
| OWNER's AFTER-TAX INCOME | | 29,000 | |

--------------------------------------------------------------------------

Total contribution  to Net Worth of Owner:

Company Growth 51,000

Take-home Salary 20,000

Take-home Profit <u>9,000</u>

OWNER's TRUE AFTER-TAX INCOME $ <u>80,000</u>

The total of your necessary costs is $208,000, leaving you with $60,000 to spend as you wish. This $60,000 is the surplus which you and your employees have created over what you and they were paid. Here is the money produced by the Secret Source--the workers. This is the true company profit.

The company profit of $60,000 is 22% of your Net Sales, a typical figure for large corporations. You should try to better with your small, efficient, well-managed company.

This $60,000 profit is money you could take home if you wished to. You would be unwise to do so. Now that you have a company going, you should use the profit for growth. The dramatic effect of such use of profit is shown in a later chapter. It will make your wealth grow at a rate that will astound you and your neighbors.

Do not report that profit to the Internal Revenue Service. Spend it first. At least most of it. Leave a little to keep the revenuers from getting nervous, and to spend for capital equipment.

Your $1,000,000 company shown here spent $51,000 for growth, leaving $9,000 as reported income after taxes (Remember that the tax was paid at the top of this Earnings Statement.)

At the bottom of the "worksheet" column you will see the tax and the before-tax income you will report-a total of $46,000 on which you paid a tax of $17,000 after including all your exemptions, deductions, and so forth on your 1040 tax fern.

Your real, factual, income requires a different calculation. You drew a salary of $20,000. The company profit on the bottom line was $9,000--which is in your profit. In addition, you reinvested for growth the amount $51,000. Your total income, the which was added to you personal worth, was $80,000. This is the income a millionaire might receive after taxes by investing his million and taking care to minimize his taxes. You are a small-business millionaire.

You can complain to your employees and your customers that your profits are only three percent of your sales ($9,000 on sales of $285,000).

As a member of your local Chamber of Commerce, you can give money to a campaign to warn the American public of the dangers of low and falling corporation profits. That expense will be tax-deductible.

With a little skill and attention, you will be able to keep your profits so low that, with the help of a few other tricks, you will pay hardly any income tax. This will give you an advantage over your competitors who haven't read this book.

## Action

1. Make your personal Earnings and Balance Sheet Statements.

2. Fill in your target $1,000,000 company financial statements if you prefer your own figures or if you can be more specific about your own company .

3. Examine the first year Earnings Statement of Hewlett-Packard. What item is missing? Did they really make a profit? Where are their salaries? Always include your own or a manager's salary on your statements .

4. Go back and see if you understand how company growth is owner income.

# 4 - The Truths About Your Profits

## The First Truth – Profit is NOT the Goal

The famous, Nobel-prize-winning and vocal economist and expert on money, Professor Milton Friedman, has asserted that business' only reason for being is to generate profits for shareholders.

Kenneth Mason, the president of the Quaker Oats Company, tells us the first truth about profits:

*"I know of no greater disservice to American business in my lifetime than Milton Friedman's widely publicized assertion that business' only reason for being is to generate profits for shareholders.*

*"What a dreary and demeaning view of the role of business and business leaders in our society!*

*"Making a profit is no more the purpose of a corporation than getting enough to eat is the purpose of life. Getting enough to eat is a requirement of life. Life's purpose, one would hope, is somewhat broader and more challenging. Likewise with business and profit."*

Profit, at least long-run break-even, is essential to the survival of a business. It is not the purpose of the business.

The purpose of your business is to produce something of value to the people. If it does not do so, it should be shut down. It is a misuse of natural resources and a misuse of the labor of its employees. The public will shut it down in due course by refusing to buy its useless product.

Let's you and I shed, once and for all, this foolish myth that the goal of business is to make a profit. The error is common enough even among economists, bankers, and businessmen who have not yet stopped to think.

You know that a business cannot operate for long with a loss. If the money flowing out exceeds the money flowing in, the business must soon close its doors. This does not mean that the purpose, the goal, is profit. Making a profit is necessary to reach the goal – and to survive.

A football team's offense works to gain yards. Its goal is plainly marked by posts on the field. Its "goal" is not the gaining of yards. But gaining yards is necessary to reach the goal. Like those yards, profit is necessary to reach the goal but it is not the goal.

## The Second Truth – the Size of Profits

The public thinks that corporation profits are 20% to 50%. Polls have repeatedly shown this to be the perception of the majority of the people.

The public perceives that businesses are growing, that they have money to buy one another, that the banks are putting luxurious buildings on every street corner, and that company owners are getting rich.

The profit the public perceives is not the profit shown on the financial statements. It is not the profit reported to the income-tax collector.

Here are some conventional profit figures for various kinds of business, as published by a businessman's magazine, Dun's Review:

| TYPE OF BUSINESS | PROFIT (percentage of sales) |
|---|---|
| Dairy Products | 1.10 |
| Bakery Products | 1.86 |
| Office and Store Fixtures | 2.32 |
| Amusement & Sporting Goods | 3.20 |
| Confectionery | 3.43 |
| Auto Parts, Accessories | 4.14 |
| Special Industry Machinery | 4.58 |
| Laboratory Instruments | 4.59 |
| Cutlery, Hand Tools, Hardware | 4.79 |
| Communication Equipment | 4.79 |
| Books, Publishing, Printing | 5.03 |

The Profit on the bottom line of the Financial Statement is the smallest figure on the statement. The Sales is the top figure, and the largest. By reporting the profit as a percentage of sales, a low number is reported. It is customary to use this number to make profits look low. There is no other special significance of this way of advertising profit.

A better measure of profit would be the increase in the net worth of the company owners. This should then be divided by the owner's investment to get a fair percentage measure of profits. Neither the total benefits of the owners nor their actual investment is easily determined.

One measure of owner benefit is the stock market value plus the dividends received. Over the last 37 years the sum of the increase in stock- market value and the dividends adds up to an annual profit to the owner of shares of corporations of 10.4%.

This 10.4% is the average of 500 companies listed by Standard and Poors and includes only well- established corporations. They are not representative of small companies, such as yours. The owner's profits in smaller and newer companies are much larger.

It is noticeable in the list at the left that the profits are lowest in those businesses that are the most stable--those that deal in necessities. Because of the steadiness of these businesses, their managers can keep the profits low without danger of slipping one year into a loss.

The control of profits at a minimum is necessary. Excess profits invite competition. Half of such profits go to the government as tax. If the money is spent for growth, the government doesn't get it.

It is not practical to operate at exactly a zero profit. In a bad year your company might then be forced into a loss. This would worry you--and your shareholders, if any.

A persistent loss could, of course, drain the company's capital, stop its growth, and finally kill the company. The ideal is to operate at a very low and steady profit. Managers have learned to do this very well, as the profit figures in the list above show.

It is because of the increasing ability of managers to control their profits that profits have been steadily decreasing during the many years of stable and growing economy since 1945.

Real profit is much greater than the reported profit. Real profit is the surplus of money from sales after all necessary costs have been paid. These costs are those incurred in selling, producing, and delivering the product. The costs of developing the product are necessary. The costs of developing additional products are not necessary.

## Real profit is the money that the manager can spend as he sees fit.

The manager must pay the costs of selling and delivering the company's products. He can decide as he sees fit how money is spent to make the company grow. These decisions are rarely revealed in the company's financial statements, except for a few incomplete items.

One estimate of the real profits can be made by adding the reported profits to the growth rate. This assumes that the money spent for growth is 100% efficient. It is not, particularly in large companies.

Large corporations are wasteful. They misspend money because the top managers cannot possibly know what is going on--the company is too big.

Assuming a realistic efficiency of 50%, the true profit is the reported profit plus twice the growth rate.

For example, the Band-Aid company, Johnson and Johnson, reported a profit of 8.5% on sales and has consistently had a growth rate of 18% per year.

Such a well-managed corporation as Johnson and Johnson is probably quite efficient--for a giant company. You can do better with your small company.

Here is how the growth of Johnson and Johnson may have been financed, although it doesn't show in its financial statements:

| | |
|---|---|
| Profit reported | 8.5 % |
| Paid dividends | 3.5 |
| Reinvested | 5 |
| Profit not reported | 31 |
| Total real profit | 36 |
| efficiency = 1/2 | |
| Growth rate, actual | 18 % |

The data is inadequate and the calculation can be criticized. The essential point remains: True profits are far greater than what is reported. In your company you will have all the facts--and all the profits.

## How To Make Hidden Profits

You can operate your company in either of two ways. You can make as much profit as possible then invest that profit in your company to make it grow. Or you can spend money for growth, increase your costs, show a small profit, and get rich.

GETTING RICH QUICKER

|  | High-Profit Method | | $1,000,000 Method |
|---|---|---|---|
| Sales | $ 285,000 | | $ 285,000 |
| Necessary costs | -188,000 | | -188,000 |
| True profit | 97,000 | | 97,000 |
| Growth reinvest | 000,000 | difference | -51,000 |
| Reported Earnings | 97,000 | | 46,000 |
| Income tax | -41,000 | | -17,000 |
| After-tax profit | 56,000 | | 29,000 |
| Owner's salar | -20,000 | | -20,000 |
| Company profit | 36,000 | | 9,000 |
| Growth reinvest | 36,000 | | +51,000 |
| Owner's salary | +20,000 | | +20,000 |
| Owner's income | 56,000 | result | 80,000 |

In the first example, the reported earnings were maximized. As a result, the income tax was also maximized.

The high tax left $56,000 to be used for the owner's (or manager's) salary and only $56,000 to be reinvested for growth.

The second case reduced the reported earnings to $46,000. The income was thereby cut to $17,000 and $29,000 was left for the owner/manager.

In the second case there was $51,000 reinvested for growth. The second case is the millionaire's way.

Counting salary, company profit, and money reinvested, the millionaire has an income of $80,000. The high-profit owner has an income of only $56,000.

The difference is even greater than it appears. As a later chapter shows, keeping your profits in the company will give you a real money bomb. Your wealth will increase explosively.

But there is a problem.

You can't buy heavy Capital equipment buildings, or land with the $51,000 you would like to reinvest.

Long-life things are not expenses on your Earnings Statement for tax purposes. They are not used up in the year in which they are purchased. Their cost must be spread over their life. Only the interest on money borrowed for such purchases and the depreciation and maintenance of such properties can be charged as expenses.

Use your company's after-tax profit for capital expenditures. Borrow--to buy the largest items, especially land and buildings--but only if necessary.

Spend your before-tax growth money on the development of new products. Develop another product line. ADVERTISE. Use the capital facilities you already have, but on added new products. Keep your fixed costs to a minimum--learn about fixed costs in the next chapter.

Small items may be purchased and charged as expenses. It is customary and permissible to write off all small items as expenses because it is not practical to keep track of them as capital. This is true even if they have a long life.

Small hand tools are not classed as capital items. They get lost too easily. Usually a company sets a rule such as "over $200 is capital." Items costing less are charged as expenses. With such a rule you can buy small things and assemble them into a big machine. The pieces and labor are expenses--a part of your $51,000 of growth expenses. But if the machine is too well built, the Internal Revenue collectors may claim that it's capital.and disallow the expense, increase your profit, raise your tax, and make you less rich.

Things can get complicated, you see. When your company is growing and making a lot of money, you will have accountants to fix your books, honestly of course.

# Action

1. Write down the goals of your business. (Profit is not a goal.)

2. Using the ideas in this book, plan how to insure that your company makes a profit so it can reach its goals.

3. Make separate lists of the expense and capital investment items for your company. Set up separate accounts for each.

4. Study the two ways of reinvesting in your company--before or after reporting earnings. Plan the best way to reinvest for growth.

# 5 - The Value of Your Company

## and How it Will Grow

You are on your way to being a millionaire. You have title to a company. This title is money. You can print "shares" and spend them just as you would any money. When the title to your company increases in value, the increase in value is in- come for you. You do not need to pay income tax on that income--only a capital gains tax and that only if you sell the company. Your employees will be the source of your income. You will reinvest their surplus so as to make your company grow.

Now you need to know how a company acquires value. You may be surprised to learn that making a profit is not even necessary to make your company valuable. You may be surprised to learn that your company's value will not be dependent upon owning a building or land or equipment. You may be surprised to learn that a company may be worth a million dollars even though it has little Book Value or Net Worth.

The first thing to do is to see how any company gets value. For this, we can look at how people who buy companies decide what to pay. The buyer will decide the value if you sell your company or if you incorporate your company and sell shares of common stock.

Some buyers of common stock want dividends. As an investment alternative to bank accounts and bonds, the value of a company depends upon the dividends paid or expected in the future. You should not pay dividends. Spend the earnings for growth before taxes for growth expenses, after taxes for capital equipment. Then sell your company to buyers who want growth. They pay more than do dividend investors.

Hewlett-Packard paid its first dividend twenty-five years after its founding, and still pays modest dividends. Every one of those first twenty-five years was profitable. By the time the company paid its first dividend, the founders were each worth at least $50,000,000. Don't pay dividends and get rich quicker.

The lesson to you, the owner of a small business that has no stockholders, is that you should not take home your profits. Leave profits in the company where they are safe from the tax collectors and will make your wealth grow.

Your company will be valuable because it makes money for the owner--or may do so in the future. Your company can make money by surviving and growing, even if it doesn't make a profit. Of course, persistent losses will deplete your company's assets. To survive, your company must break even over the long run, but you do not need to make a profit every month--or even every year.

## Profit and Company Value

To learn what a losing company might be worth, I went through the June 1978 Standard & Poor's Stock Guide and listed the companies that were in the red. Of the first 500 companies listed, 55 reported losses. Taking the last price of the shares and the number of shares outstanding, the total market value of these 55 losing companies was $1,260,000,000. There is a market value of greater than $10 billion for all the large companies that are losing money.

A company is a thing of value, even if it's losing money. I'm not recommending that you deliberately own a loser. It's better to make a profit. You can sleep better, pay your bills on time, and borrow money more easily when a rapid increase in sales requires more cash. For you to be a millionaire, you can own either a small and profitable company or a larger and losing company. Profitable is easier to sleep with.

Here is a graph of the market value of companies versus their reported earnings. You can see that there is little relation between the value of a company and its profit. The losing companies grouped at the left seem to be valued as if they were profitable. Many losing companies are worth more than profitable companies of the same size.

A loser with hope is worth more than a winner without dreams.

You have good reason to wonder what makes a losing company valuable. If it is not profits, if profits are not even necessary, then makes a company valuable? You may think Assets or Net Worth are the answer. Let's examine these for a relation to the value of your company.

## Company Value is Not in Profit

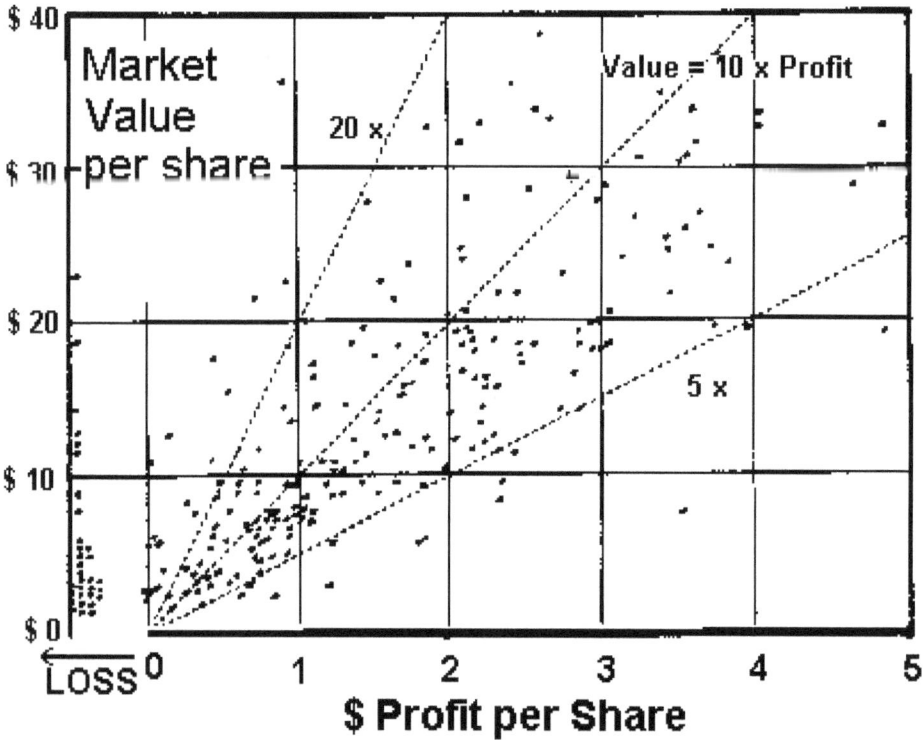

## Book Value and Company Value

When we think of company value, our first thought after Profits may be Book Value--it sounds right. Surely the books must mean something. The stockholders in the Penn Central holding company must have thought so. Some of them paid $80 per share when the Book Value was $116 per share and the Net Worth was almost three billion dollars. In fact, the company was on the verge of bankruptcy and the stock- holders got a dollar or two for their shares after the bankruptcy became certain. The Book Value did them no good. Book Value means nothing.

Net worth, commonly called Book Value, is a number which balances the Balance Sheet, nothing more. It is the difference between two large numbers, one of which (Assets) is largely a figment of "generally accepted accounting principles," not a reality. Buildings and equipment may have been depreciated too slowly and be worn out while still nor low. Look at the scatter of on the books--like the tracks

## COMPANY VALUE IS NOT BOOK VALUE

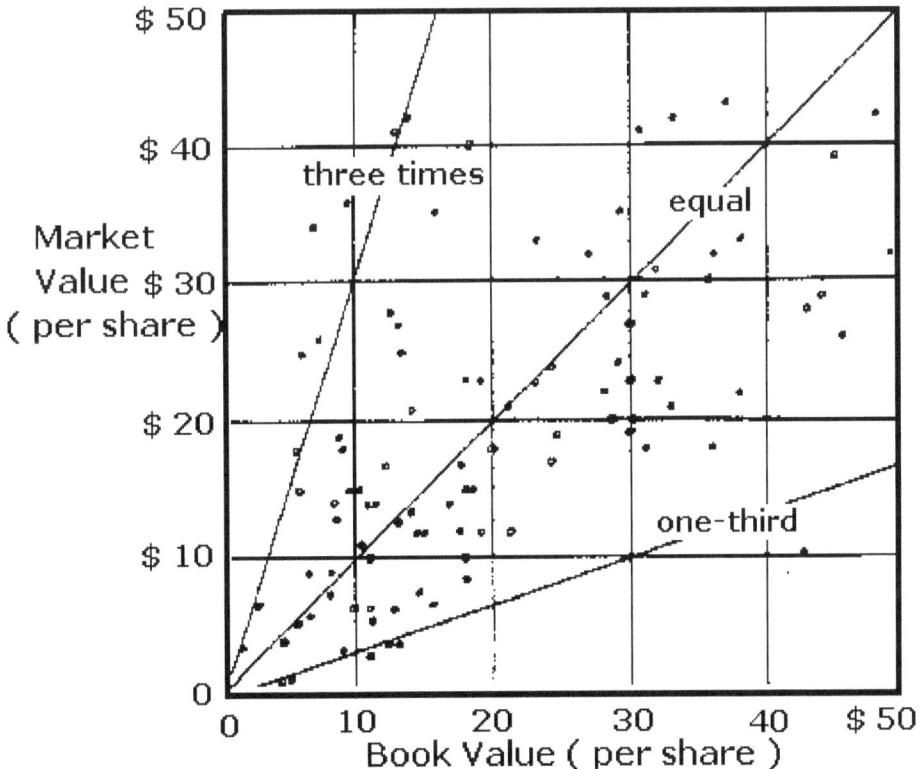

Market Value $ (per share) vs Book Value (per share), with lines labeled "three times", "equal", and "one-third".

of the Penn Central, whose maintenance was not a part of the grand plan of the railroad management. High profits will increase your Net Worth and hurt your company.

You will see here a graph showing lack of relation between the Net Worth or Book Value and the market price of a company. This is a random stocks in the fall of 1976 when the stock market was neither high now low. Look at the scatter of points. The market does not depend on the Book Value. The price of the shares ranges from five times the Book Value to one-fifth of that value. For example, if you know the Book Value of a company is $10 per share, the share scatter of points suggest that the market value of the shares may be anywhere from $3 to $30. It is futile to give your company a high Net Worth in the hope that it will sell for a higher price. There must be something else that makes your company valuable.

## Employees and Company Value

What is one employee worth to you? We have learned that employees must be the source of company owners' wealth. It is they who create the surplus of profits over your necessary costs. They are always paid much less than they produce. The extra production is at your disposal. You will use it to make your company grow (and hire more employees). You will use it for buying more capital equipment after you pay your income taxes. You will have some left over for your own pocket money. Surely such a source of wealth must have value.

In fact, the average market value of a company of the kind that you own is about $40,000 per employee. This is a conservative figure in these days of a giant government devaluing the dollar. The figure varies from industry to industry. It is higher for small companies, which are more efficient than the giants. It is lower for retail stores, whose employees too often do too little work. It is higher for well-managed retail stores that have a system and have employees that work.

1999 NOTE: The $40,000 figure was determined by looking at small companies in 1980. The number would be higher today. But the principle is the thing here and time has made all numbers rise, but has not altered the principle: employees are valuable. It is also a fact that since 1980 wages have not kept up with productivity so employees are more valuable – but not paid more.

For a company making small, technological things, the figure is higher. The value of Hewlett-Packard has ranged from $40,000 to $90,000 per employee. In 1980 they have 55,000 employees and a market value of about $3.7 billion. This is a company value of about $67,000 per employee.

A company with 25 employees should be worth $1,000,000. This $40,000 "rule-of-thumb" will give you a good idea of the worth of any business. But the value depends upon how you manage your company, and sometimes on the whims of the company marketplace.

Let's look at some examples of the actual values of some companies.

In the Statistical Abstracts of the United States, we learn that in 1976 the average manufacturing employee produced $59,000 and was paid wages of $10,500. Allowing for fringe benefits of $2,500, they produced a surplus of $26,000 apiece. What would you be willing to pay for a machine that produced such a surplus over what it cost?

The average retail worker sells about $40,000 per year of goods which were purchased wholesale for about $20,000. With total wages and fringe benefits amounting to $7,000, they produced a surplus of only $15,000--half that of a manufacturing worker. Do not expect to be worth a million with 25 employees in a retail store. Plan to have a chain of stores or franchises. In a later chapter you will learn to SELL franchises--not to buy one.

Suppose you "own" a manufacturing employee. He or she will produce a surplus or true profit for you of about $26,000 each year. This is equivalent to your having invested the sum of $525,000 at 8% interest. Having employees is like having money. Having employees is as good as having savings in the bank. Use your employees' surplus to expand your company and get more employees.

To be sure of being able to sell your company for $1,000,000, you should have about 25 employees worth $40,000 apiece. You do not need so large a company to just live like a millionaire. Ten or fourteen employees should be enough.

The reason you need a bigger company if you are going to sell it and retire is that owning a company gives you certain privileges you will lose when you sell. The owner of a company has privileges which are worth a great amount of money. A company with as few as seven employees might allow you to live like a millionaire.

A company of 25 employees, after being sold for $1,000,000 will do the same for you when you retire.

*When my friend, Bob Denman, was making his product in his garage and had no employees, he took no vacations and worked 14 hours a day and seven days a week. All of his travel and entertainment expenses came out of his own pocket. He didn't travel much. When he had a few employees he worked less, traveled when he wanted, and entertained out of the company expense account (tax deductible). Now, with 43 employees, he is long past the $1,000,000 mark. His employees make him worth two million and the government pays half of all his personal expenses that he can relate to his business. Rather than sell, he is turning the management of his company over to his employees and living the life a millionaire deserves. You can do the same.*

*But don't do what Dan Newcomb did. I was asked to invest in his company and studied it thoroughly. He had an excellent consumer product: needed, offering outstanding features, easy to sell for a profitable price. His prospectus showed that he had a sales rate of $85,621" per year and expected to have a rate of $119,544 in the next quarter. He offered a part of the corporation at a price that corresponded to a total value of $240,000. Because the company could grow rapidly, this price was reasonable. I didn't invest. No one else would. The company went out of business. The reason: there were no employees. Dan did everything himself. He had not learned to use employees. A company is a group of employees--that's what the word "company" means. Employees are the source of wealth.*

The free enterprise system is the best system for employees, even though it makes employers rich. The surplus the employees create goes mostly back into company growth and more jobs.

More jobs means more competition among employers to hire good people, and this means higher wages. Other systems (socialist, communist, fascist) harm the workers. Because their government planning and operation of the economy is ineffective, the standard is lower under such systems. Because such governments must control everything, there is little freedom.

Free enterprise lets people be free, provided only that they have jobs. You can help by having more employees.

## Employees – the Source of Wealth

The small entrepreneur--you--works in a world of land, buildings, equipment, people, and ideas. Money is only a mechanism for trading among these things. The new entrepreneur with a good idea is short of these things he needs to run his business.

He wants a business of his own and the wealth-and satisfaction it can bring him. He has no interest in tricky theories of economics by Marx, Mao Tse Tung, Friedman, Clark, or the Federal Reserve. He just wants a way into the millionaire's system.

Land, buildings, and equipment require more money than he has. But people come in small pieces. They can be "rented" by the hour. They ask for only half of what they produce. People--employees--are the secret source of wealth.

Employees in manufacturing cost about $16,000 per year (in 1979), including their fringe benefits. We need data showing what they are worth to their employer. Here are the 20 smallest of a list of 100 small, growing companies compiled by the magazine, INC. The market value is the summer 1979 stock-market quotation.

| | Sales $ M | Employees | Company Sales (per employee) | Value |
|---|---|---|---|---|
| Osmonics | $ 3.0 | 75 | $ 40,213 | $ 98,700 |
| Sonic Development | 3.1" | 40 | 76,300 | 67,500 |
| Techtran Industries | 3.1" | 79 | 39,190 | |
| Nutrition World | 4.2 | 160 | 26,344 | |
| LRC | 4.3 | 114 | 37,544 | 64,900 |
| Teleconcepts | 4.4 | 47 | 92,957 | |
| Time Sharing Resources | 4.6 | 80 | 57,975 | 63,800 |
| Tratec | 5.2 | 92 | 56,783 | |
| Galaxy Oil ** | 5.9 | 44 | 134,182 | 434,900 |
| Gallon Petroleum ** | 6,8 | 39 | 173,846 | |
| Norstan | 6.8 | 225 | 30,427 | 42,200 |
| Raycomm Industries | 7.3 | 304 | 23,937 | 4,600 |
| Custom Alloy | 7.6 | 191 | 39,618 | 14,100 |
| Med General | 8.3 | 148 | 56,047 | 182,000 |
| Dranetz Engineering Labc | 8.4 | 102 | 46,132 | 76,400 |
| Par Systems | 8.6 | 218 | 39,596 | 36,700 |
| Compact Video Systems | 8.7 | 169 | 51,651 | 141,000 |
| Salem National | 8.8 | 139 | 63,165 | 33,000 |
| Thermal Industries | 9.9 | 470 | 21,162 | |
| Modular Ambulance | 11.4 | 168 | 69,101 | |

The average amount of sales per employee is $48,230 (leaving out the two oil companies. Oil companies are special cases.) The stock market also places odd values on "timely new idea" companies. Med General and Compact Video Systems are such companies. Perhaps you should build a company based on a new idea.

(Get current information before you invest in any of these companies .)

If the sales per employee are too low, you can't pay the employees and your company will be in trouble. Except for the oil companies, the average market value of these twenty companies is 77$44,517 per employee--about equal to their sales.

Is this a real relationship or is it a coincidence? Are the employees the secret source of wealth or is capital the source? The economists sometimes argue the point, but economists don't run businesses. To get the facts we must go to a large, stable well-known corporation that publishes the data we need. Let's see what such a company says about its source of wealth.

Johnson & Johnson, the Band-Aid company, famous for its quality medical products, tells us their 1978 costs in a way we can use to determine the value of employees. They tell us the number and the cost of their employees.

| | **Johnson & Johnson** | | Percentage of sales | |
|---|---|---|---|---|
| SALES | | | | |
| Gross | $ 5,514,564,000 | | 100% | |
| less income tax | 215,156,000 | $ 5,199,408,000 | 6 | 94% |
| COSTS | | | | |
| Employees (67,000) | 1,101,585,000 | | 31 | |
| Material & Services | 1,687,575,000 | | 48 | |
| Capital | 311,907,000 | $ 3,101,063,000 | 9 | 88% |
| NET EARNINGS RETAINED | | $ 198,545,000 | | 6% |

The 67,000 employees cost an average $16,442 per year, including all their fringe benefits: pensions, insurance, social security, and so forth. They produce sales of $52,456 apiece. Those sales pay for the material and services Johnson & Johnson buys to produce the product and run the plants. The sales also pay for the capital, which doesn't cost much.

The company costs have three components: employees, materials and services, and capital. The materials and services do not **produce** wealth--they **are** wealth. They are produced by employees and capital in some other companies: the suppliers.

Can the capital be the source of the wealth? If the $788 million of property, plant, and equipment owned by Johnson & Johnson were invested at 10%,.it would produce $78.8 million, which would be only 26.5% of the earnings they report. The employees deserve credit for at least 75.7% of the net earnings.

The stock market, in recent years, has valued Johnson & Johnson at about $ 4,184,000,000. This a value of $62,448 per employee. Using the division between capital and labor that gives labor credit for only 75.7% of the earnings gives the employees a value of $46,024. Our rule-of-thumb of $40,000 seems reasonable and conservative.

> 1999 NOTE: This was based on data available in 1980. The value of employees is probably more today. Furthermore, worker's wages have not kept up with their productivity so the owner gets to keep more

A giant company, such as Johnson & Johnson, as good as it is, is less efficient than your small company. Furthermore, the figure used here for the market value of Johnson & Johnson reflects a historically low stock-market value for the company, compared to its earnings and number of employees.

Out of its capital and employees, Johnson & Johnson creates wealth. The company is worth four billion dollars. This wealth was produced mostly by its employee's labor; only to a small extent by their capital. The employees are the Secret Source of wealth. They take home as pay about half of what they product. The rest is in the hands of the company owners, who spend their wealth in many ways, including, if they wish, as capital in their company or in other companies. Too many men who start businesses do not know this. You can develop your company better, more quickly, and for more wealth for yourself because you know where the wealth comes from.

If your little company runs like Johnson & Johnson, here it is:

---

**YOUR $1,000,000 COMPANY**

| | | | Percent of sales |
|---|---|---|---|
| SALES | | | |
| Gross | $ 285,000 | | 100 % |
| less income tax | 17,442 | $ 267,558 | 6 %  94 % |
| COSTS | | | |
| Employees  (5.4) | 89,319 | | 31 % |
| Material & Services | 136,857 | | 48 % |
| Capital | 25,292 | $ 251,468 | 9 %  88 % |
| NET EARNINGS RETAINED | | $ 16,090 | 6 % |
| Owner's salary 20,000 7 | | | |
| Increase in company's value | | $ 43,910 | 15 % |
| OWNER'S TOTAL INCOME . . . . . . . . | | $ 80,000 | 28 % |

---

Remember that the Retained Earnings can be spent for capital equipment and is not the only money retained in the company. Expenses for growth: development of new products, advertising to increase sales, additional employees, are all included in "Costs." For this reason the increase in the company's value is several times the Net Earnings Retained.

Your employees will produce more than the Retained Earnings indicate. Most of the excess they produce will be spent by you before it reaches the bottom line of your Earnings Statement. What reaches the bottom line will be half taken by the government as income tax. Have employees and spend the money.

Employees alone are not enough to make you rich. Your employees must have something to do, and A PLACE TO DO IT. They must produce some thing or they must provide some service.

There needs to be A PRODUCT. The product may be new or old. It may be patented or commonplace.

Your company must also have A WAY OF DOING BUSINESS. You may manufacture or you may distribute or you may retail. You may invent products or you may trade them. You may sell your products by mail order or you may own retail stores. There must be a way of doing that business, not just any way, but a way that characterizes your company.

There must be an INCOME. Someone must pay your company for its products or services. There must be SALES. There must be CUSTOMERS. Something which someone regards as valuable must change hands for money. It is quite remarkable how many business owners ignore some one necessary ingredient.

There is one more ingredient that will you need to become a millionaire. While a company can exist without it, that company will not make you rich.

That essential factor in the millionaire's company is GROWTH. It is growth that provides you with that hidden income that will make you rich without paying taxes. If you ever sell your company, a record of growth and the prospect of continued growth will make your company more saleable and for a higher price.

The next chapter tells of the method used by America's millionaire company owners to make their companies grow.

## Action

1. Compare your company's value with its book value and with its profit.

2. Compare your company's value with the rule of "$40,000 per employee." Does it differ from the rule? Why? If it is low, learn from this book what you can do to raise its value. (Don't forget to count the manager, perhaps you, as one employee.)

3. Compare your company's figures with those percentage relations based on Johnson & Johnson on the previous page.

# 6 – Your $1,000,000 Money Bomb

## Your Company Can Explosively Make You Rich

The littlest, faltering company has the potential of making its owner a millionaire. A company that Costs little to start and little to run has the greatest potential. If little money is needed to start, little money is needed to grow. A company that needs little money to run can stay out of the hands of bankers and speculators. You can retain ownership, avoid financial risk, control your company, and get rich. What you need to know is how to finance the growth.

## $1,000,000 Starting from Nickels

Many, perhaps most, of America giant companies started small, in someone's house, garage, or basement. The Mattel toy company was started at home--making dolls. Hewlett-Packard started in Bill Hewlett's small garage. Firestone started in Firestone's kitchen where he cooked rubber on the kitchen stove. The examples are endless. You don't need to own a giant corporation.

You can start your small company on the growth path. If you start getting too rich, you can get out. The rate at which you get rich may amaze you.

In three years, Wally "Famous" Amos grew a $3,000,000 business with 100 employees. His product is a cookie: a chocolate-chip cookie. People don't want cheap cookies. They buy his high-priced cookies as fast as he and his 100 employees can make them. Wally Amos was surprised when he got rich.

He tells us he "just wanted to make a living." Surprise by riches is common among millionaires who didn't know the secret source of wealth.

Most American millionaires were surprised when they found themselves getting rich. They just wanted to make a living. They hired more employees without knowing that employees are the Secret Source of wealth. You have the advantage of knowing. You can plan the growth of your company better and get rich quicker.

Whether you are making an established company grow or starting a new company, you may have to depend on money from sales to purchase the materials and labor you need to make the next lot of product. As fast as the customers pay, you can make more product or undertake to perform more services. Later you can show your books to your banker and get money to speed up the process--but you will not need to.

When Hewlett and Packard were starting their billion-dollar company, they had to pay cash. An acquaintance of mine, the president of a company, told me how Dave Packard would come to his plastics company with cash in hand to buy knobs for his instruments, his product. Dave Packard took his knobs in a brown paper bag back to Hewlett's garage to make more instruments; to pay for more knobs.

Using income to finance the next production is called "bootstrap" financing. By this method a company can grow "with no visible means of support." It grows with no outside money, no bankers, no investors, with the founder/owner keeping the company entirely under his control. The owner increases his wealth. The rate of increase can be explosive.

The sales pride of your product will be about twice the necessary production cost.

---

1999 NOTE:

The idea that the price of a good may be twice the cost of producing it perturbs people who don't know the facts of business. This ignorance may lead a new businessman to underprice his product.

An example: the cost of a vehicle is much higher than most business owners realize. 2015 note added: the manufacturing cost of this book is $2.65. It is underpriced.

---

Bootstrapping – investing your profits -- can make your company grow beyond your wildest dreams. Dave Packard remarked that when he and Bill reached sales of ten million, he thought that was it: a great success in creating company and big enough. Only later did he realize they were on a growth path they could ride to billions.

# THE WHEELS OF YOUR COMPANY

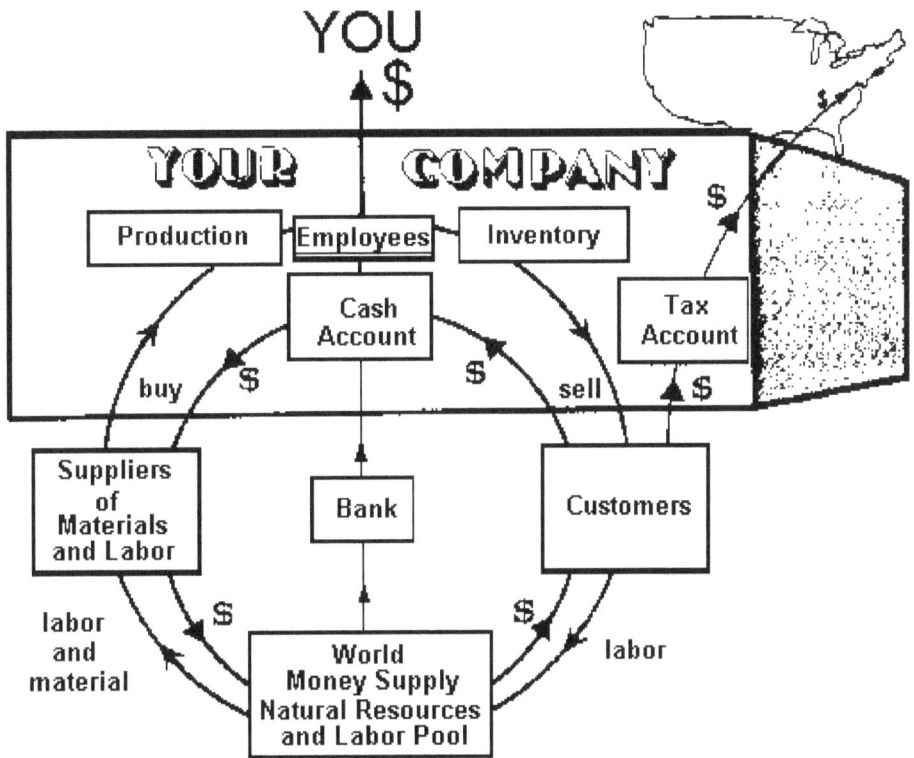

Your company has two wheels. One carries cash in one direction. The other carries materials, labor, and your product in the other direction. The outer wheel starts with your first production--either product or service.  Production goes into inventory, then to the customer.

The inner wheel circulates money. Your customers put money into your cash account, and into your tax account. With the money, you buy more material and labor. You are a tax collector. Let your accounting department pay the taxes from the money your customers pay you. Set your prices up to furnish this money. Don't worry about taxes. You don't pay them. You just collect them.

Companies collect taxes from their customers and deliver the taxes to the government. The tax-collection function has nothing to do with the operation of your company, except that your bookkeeper or you must transfer the money from your customers to the government.

A later chapter discusses taxes in detail.

But is out of date in its details. Tax laws are always changing but the general principles have not been changing.

The amount of your company's income tax is based on your profit. You will collect more taxes than you need to if you let your profits get too high. If you collect more taxes from your customers than do your competitors, your price will be higher and you may lose business.

Keep your profits as low as possible, but have enough control so that you can quickly make adjustments and show a small profit in each month. In a later chapter you will learn how to keep your costs controllable. One important controllable cost is the cost of advertising. Advertising is too often neglected and needs special attention.

## Advertising – Your Company Locomotive

Mr. Wrigley, of chewing-gum fame, was asked why he advertised so much when he was already selling more gum than anyone else. He explained: "Advertising is the locomotive that pulls the train. When the locomotive is running smoothly, the passengers don't even know it's there. If the locomotive stops, the passengers know it immediately."

It is advertising that makes the wheels of cash and product rotate. Somehow, one way or another, your customers must learn that you have a product which they should buy. When business is good, it's easy to fall into the trap of cutting your advertising expenses. Nothing is more dangerous than to stop advertising either because business is too good or to cut costs when business is bad.

*An acquaintance of mine had a thriving hearing-aid business. He sold it. The new owner saw that business was good, so he stopped advertising. In just a few months his business was in trouble. He didn't understand why and begged my friend to come back and help him.*

Advertising may well be the first step in starting a business. Many businesses have been started by first running an ad to see if anyone wants the product. When there is a good response, the entrepreneur apologized for the slow delivery, finished his product design, and started production.

*My friend, Bob Denman, started making a product in his garage. To build sales, he visited schools and donated free samples for the students to use. Later, the students went into industry and ordered the product they had learned to use. The advertising paid off, a million dollars plus in fact.*

To make a million you have to get out to the customer. As Denman says, "no bee ever got honey by staying in the hives."

While advertising is the engine that makes the wheels turn, it is the employees who do the work and generate the surplus for you. If you get things set up right, you do not need to be present at all in your company. Just collect the money.

*In my town there is a book store. On the last Friday of the month the owner makes an appearance. He looks the place over, collects the money, and disappears. He has his employees in place to both manage and operate the company.*

You now know the source of the book-store owner's monthly check: his employees. You may wonder how he got so many employees that he no longer needs to work. He has a very large bookstore. To be

a millionaire in retail, this is what you need. But, the question then is:
how does any business get so big? You see many businesses around

# THE MILLIONAIRE'S METHOD
## Positive Feedback -- Bootstrap Financing

your town that never grow. There must be a secret of growth which
they don't know about.

The secret of growth is feedback, POSITIVE FEEDBACK. You
saw an illustration of positive feedback in the table that showed how
a sale could pay the costs of a larger sale--and so on for rapid growth
Production leads FORWARD TO sales. Sales FEED BACK MONEY
to finance larger production.

But that is only one of the ways the idea of positive feedback can
make your company grow. If you understand positive feedback, you
will not take home as much profit, but you will get rich quicker.

POSITIVE FEEDBACK -- THE GROWTH SECRET

The drawing shows the feedback paths of your company. The heart
of your company is the "total necessary cost." This is the cost of
keeping your business going without growth and without profit.

After subtracting your necessary costs from your gross sales, there
remains the gross profit or "employees' surplus." The gross profit is
used for many things: cost reduction, quality improvement, advertising,
and new product development. These uses should be sufficient to
absorb almost all of the gross profit and keep it out of the hands of the
government.

Positive feedback is explosive. A bomb is an example of positive feedback. A slow fire in a closed place heats itself and speeds up the rate of burning. The faster burning raises the temperature higher and again speeds up the burning. As the fire spreads more heat is fed back and the thing blows up. Positive feedback makes bombs. You can have a money bomb.

If the output increases the input, there is positive feedback. For example, if the profit of your company is used to increase advertising and increase the input (the sales), the output is increasing the input. There is then more output (profit) to pay for more advertising. And so on.

Advertising is not the only way to use positive feedback. You can use your output to develop new products, to increase the quality of your products, and for cost-reduction measures. Each of these uses of profit will increase your profit. Remember to spend your profit before it shows--before the government sees it and wants half.

As your uses of gross profit increases your sales, you will have more gross profit to use. You will be busy spending money to get more money to spend. What will happen, as you now know, is that your employees will be generating wealth. You will be using that wealth to make your company grow.

The test of good feedback is that it must produce more than it costs. An amount of money spent on quality improvement must produce more than that amount of increased gross profit. An amount of money spent on advertising must produce sales which yield more than that amount of gross profit. An amount of money spent on new products must be repaid by a larger increase in gross profit.

One of a company manager's most important jobs is to provide and to control these feedbacks. There is always the temptation to stop the feedback and take home the profits.

If you take home the profits, the government will mug you on the way home and try to take half. You will have left an immediate cash income and you won't get rich quick.

By taking your profits out you will slow the growth of your company. A company that is not growing is in danger of shrinking. Nothing stands still. A stagnant company loses value by standing still.

By Action, get  POSITIVE FEEDBACK and GROWTH

# Action

1. Estimate the "turn-around time for money in your company. How long does it take for money received from a sale to be converted into another sale?

2. How many products can you deliver for the money received from 100 sales?

3. Take action to shorten the turn-around time.

4. Take action to increase the prices of your product or service and to reduce the costs. Use quality and service as the basis for the high prices you ask.

5. Review your advertising program.

Make sure you are testing your advertising whenever possible.

Keep records of the costs and the results of each advertising effort.

6. Act immediately to improve your advertising. Make certain all of your potential customers know you exist.

7. Review the ways in which you are using your employee's surplus to make your company grow. Act to improve your feedback.

# 7 - Your Management of Company Money

```
YOUR COMPANY BULLETIN BOARD


Our business is booming.  Profits are high and rising.

Our sales volume has risen by over fifty percent this month.

Profits are up by sixty percent.

New orders have reached a record high.



We have no cash to meet the payroll Friday and must cease
operations.


Bankruptcy may allow us to restructure our financing.
```

## Cash

That is the Final Report of many a million-dollar dream company. Many fast-growing businesses face this paradox. Good and growing sales have encouraged expansion. You know that employees will make you wealthy, so you quickly hire more. They need a place to work, so you rent more space.

You buy a year's supply of material for a bargain price. Your advertising has worked well, so you order more. Everything is going great. You are getting rich quick.

Suddenly: you are out of cash, out of business, and not rich at all. You didn't know about CASH MANAGEMENT.

More companies get into trouble by running out of cash than for any other reason. A very profitable company can run out of cash. The best product is just the product most likely to deplete your cash and get you into trouble.

Cash is not the only thing you need to know about money management. You need to know about the many BREAK EVEN POINTS. Many company founders never stop to calculate their break-even points and can't understand why their company is in trouble, nor why the bank won't lend them money. You must understand break-even points--all of them.

Finally, you must know how to set the RIGHT PRICE for your product. Prices are not determined by costs or by supply-and-demand or by competition or by price-fixing or by price leadership. They are influenced by all of these--but usually set by whim.. You must strive to do a little better. Pricing requires continuous attention by the company owner, YOU.

Your American Millionaire's Method is to have employees generate a surplus for you, the owner, to re-invest. You will use feedback. The profits from each sale will pay the costs of producing many more sales. To do this requires a controlled flow of cash from your customers to your employees and suppliers. Controlling that flow of cash requires a budget.

## The Cash Budget

Of all the financial statements and budgets of a company, none is more important to a new company than the cash budget. Only if you have cash on payday, can you have employees and get rich. The cash budget is a plan to get rich.

You need a realistic cash budget. You must review your cash position weekly, if not daily. This requires that you keep up-to-date books. The more successful you are, the more necessary is the control of cash.

Positive feedback depends on a flow of cash. But the sources of cash are not always dependable. Customers can be slow to pay. Banks can back out of promised loans. Suppliers can demand cash on delivery. Explosive growth demands more and more cash, but you shouldn't have excess cash on hand, doing nothing.

If pay-day comes and you don't have cash to pay your employees, you'll lose your secret source of wealth-and it will be no secret.

I have had personal acquaintance with companies that had severe cash problems. One was a fast-growing California electronics company. The owner told me of his adventure on Wall Street, desperately seeking cash to save his profitable company. He was confronted by young Harvard Masters of Business Administration" who had no comprehension of how a small company grows. Their training had been directed to the management of giant corporations. They were mainly interested in getting a "piece of the action." He gave up in disgust, went back to Los Angeles, pulled hard on his bootstraps, and survived.

I was the first customer of a Santa Clara County "silicon valley" semiconductor equipment company. One day I received a telephone call form Wall Street (a young MBA) asking about the company, which was seeking cash.

The company was growing rapidly and running out of cash. They got it and grew into a large company. One of the things they had to do was visit their customers and ask for money.

Their newly-hired controller appeared in my office one day. He wanted to negotiate some cash for a piece of equipment they had not yet completed. We negotiated a completion schedule and a discount. In return, I went to my accounting department and got them a check for the work already completed. Without such resolutions of their cash shortage, they might not have been able to stay in business. They were growing and profitable--and in danger of not meeting their payroll.

---

1999 NOTE: The company was Applied Materials.
In 1980 I did not want to name them.

---

Profit isn't enough to insure survival. You must have cash when you need it. The smart company owner keeps a cash forecast--in his head or on paper. On paper is better:

# CASH FORECAST

(how one might look)

|  | January | February | March |
|---|---|---|---|
| Cash on hand, beginning of month | $ 700 | $ 1,200 | $ 900 |
| Cash receipts during the month | $ 4,300 | $ 5,100 | $ 6,000 |
| Total cash available | $ 5,000 | $ 6,300 | $ 6,900 |
| Cash disbursements during month | $ 3,800 | $ 5,400 | $ 7,200 |
| Net cash at end of month | $ 1,200 | $ 900 | ($ 300) |
| Loan received during month | --0 | 0 | $ 1,000 |
| Cash on hand at end of month | $ 1,200 | $ 900 | $ 700 |

Under Cash Disbursements, list some of your principal cash uses, such as these:

| Materials | Rent |
|---|---|
| Payroll | New Equipment |
| Advertising | Owner--cash draw (even owners eat) |

The forecast shown here starts with $700 cash. To this will be added receipts of $4,300 during January-if all goes according to forecast.

Only $3,800 of this will be needed during January, leaving $1,200 with which to start February.

Business is growing. New equipment will be needed in February. At the end of February there will be left only $900 with which to start March.

During March the cash disbursements are expected to exceed the available cash. Perhaps some material must be purchased in anticipation of increased sales. As a result, a loan will be necessary during March. The plan is to borrow $1,000 and end March with $700 cash on hand with which to start April.

You should make your cash forecast more detailed. So that you can see what is going on, the cash forecast and the cash report ought to provide separate items of cash use. List at least the following:

*Cash Sales*

*Collections of Accounts Receivable*

*Other Cash Sources*

Remember, receiving an order is not a receipt of cash. A loan is cash as soon as you can start spending it.

This is cash accounting, not accrual accounting. In cash management, only the-hard-stuff-in-hand counts.

In cash management there is no distinction between disbursements for expense items and for capital items.

If your net cash at the end of the month is going to be a deficit, you must arrange for a loan or some other source of cash, or cut some planned expenditure--or 80 out of business.

And don't count on a loan until you've got a firm commitment in writing. Coins in your pocket are better. A slip in cash can put you out of business faster than anything else.

There is no simple relation between your success or failure and your cash situation (unless you run out of cash). Old, stagnant companies often have excellent cash positions. They go out of business for lack of sales. Such a failing company may be awash in cash. This a sign of bad management.

A new, profitable, and rapidly-growing company may have a serious cash shortage and may fail for lack of cash in the face of high and rising profits.

Because you will have a new company and a fast-growing company, you should review your cash account each week and whenever there is a large cash transaction due. One week you may find that you are going to be short of cash next week.

## Cash When You Need Cash

Long before you need cash, you must have a plan. Either plan never to need cash except from your customers, or plan to have a loan arranged in advance.

A need for cash can arise at any time. The economic system can upset your cash planning.

*Our famous bootstrap (feedback) company, Hewlett-Packard, which avoids loans like the plague, once saw its cash position drop by twelve million dollars in three months.*

*The customers were the cause. They were suddenly slow to pay their bills. The government had tightened credit to hold back the inflation caused by deficit spending for the Vietnam war. The customers were using their suppliers as sources of cash--by withholding cash from them. The discounts for prompt payment were not enough to discourage the practice because the interest rates and rate of inflation were as high as the discounts.*

1999 NOTE: Hewlett-Packard has continued to avoid debt. But, typical of corporations, Hewlett-Packard has been in debt since its first year. Debt is good. Debt pays for long-term capital investments and is useful for cash management. At the end of October 1998, HP had a long-term debt of $ 2.063 billion. (and have in mind that it's managers are mostly Republicans). – an unwamted comment

You can need cash loans no matter how well you manage your company. You will need a reservoir of cash, either your own (company) savings-which will be growing, or a bank credit line. Plan ahead for cash.

At some point in the development of your company you should set up a "line of credit" with your bank. This simply provides that the bank commits itself to provide cash when you need it, up to a certain limit--rather like having a company credit card with a high limit. In return, you will be required to operate your company within certain financial limits, which you should do anyway.

Bank of America publishes a booklet called, "Financing Small Business." This booklet tells you what is needed to get a loan. You can get the same information from your bank in some form.

1999 NOTE: I don't know if they still do. Call them and ask.

Keep in mind that banks only do business with companies that need money--and only loan money to companies that do not need money. Try to run your company so that you do not need an emergency loan. The later chapter on small-business ownership without risk will help you do this.

A typical loan application will contain the following:

*Terms...How the money will be used, in detail. The security and the agreements as to how the company will operate (insurance carried, cash kept in the bank account, repayment schedule).*

*Resumes...The qualifications of the owner and key employees--the source of the wealth with which to repay the loan. Credit references.*

*Personal Financial Statement...The owner of a privately-held company is responsible for its debts.*

*Business Plan...A detailed description of the business, its history, its competition, its growth potential, its sales plan, its method of operation, and its capabilities.*

*Profit-and-loss Statement...Previous and projected. Balance Sheet...Current and projected.*

*Cash-Flow Statement... Previous and projected.*

If you establish credit references for your personal money and develop the required accounting statements as you go along, you will be prepared to go to your bank and get a loan when you need it.

You can get a loan even if you don't have a profit, but you must at least be able to show that you know your break-even points. Before getting to them, what about getting cash without a loan?

Rather than borrow money, you can sell a piece of your company. To do so, you must complicate the legal structure of your company. You must have a partnership or a corporation. If you sell shares, you get involved in the laws controlling the sales of securities. When you are done, you will own less of your company.

Success may force you to sell part of your company. You may need far more money than you can borrow. The trick is to get cash by selling a part of the company, but still keep firm control of your company.

You will need good and honest lawyers and accountants. Pay them for their work. Stay away from those who want part of your company in return for a few weeks work. These experts well know that the way to wealth is through owning at least a piece of a growing company.

In due time, you can share your company money with those who have made the largest contributions to the growth of your company--your key and longest employees.

To keep things under your control, to avoid being forced to give up the control of your company, you must be able to control your break-even points.

Breaking even is the secret of keeping control of a live and growing company, getting loans when you need them--if ever, and keeping yourself free of the fear of risk.


## Breaking Even – or Going Broke

Companies do not always make a profit. A new company must spend some money before it makes a sale. It starts with a loss. A company may choose to accept a loss for a time so as to be prepared for a larger profit later.

A new product being introduced by an established company will not make a profit at first. What is said here applies to such a product as well as to an entire company. The manager of the largest corporation as well as the new small-company owner must know about break-even points.

At the break-even points the price equals the costs. But there are two kinds of costs: <u>fixed</u> and <u>variable</u>.

<u>Fixed costs</u> do not depend upon the number of products made. Your rent, the cost of utilities, interest on loans and mortgages, fire insurance, and the living expenses of the company owner are fixed costs. They continue even if no products are made and no services are performed.

<u>Variable costs</u> are proportional to the number of products made. The material that goes into the products, the labor of making the products, the costs of delivering the products, these are variable. They vanish when production stops.

The fixed costs change when new plants and machines are bought. The variable costs per product change when the efficiency of labor and material use change.

You will be in trouble if your costs are mostly fixed and your sales fall off. Keep your fixed costs down and closely controlled.

Study the Break-Even Point graph carefully. You must understand it. Do not go into business if you do not understand the fixed costs, variable costs, and break-even points.

The company of the graph made a profit almost immediately, as small new companies can often do. They start with no fixed costs--using a garage or kitchen. They keep poor books, don't know about "break-even," and soon learn the hard way.

When the sales volume required it, this company rented space. A new machine was purchased. The fixed costs jumped up. The variable costs also rose until the owner's wife learned how to operate the new machine.

Once the machine was learned and the rented space efficiently arranged, the company made a fine profit and grew rapidly. The building became crowded so a new building was purchased. Again the rise in fixed costs overcame the sales and the company had a loss.

As the sales volume continued to rise, and the new plant became efficient, the company became profitable again. After this time the company never again operated at a loss.

Although the company as a whole never again had a loss, the same principles of costs, sales, and break-even applied to each new product it introduced.

At first, each new product was sold at a loss. Then the sales volume rose until a break-even point was reached. When the production was expanded by means of new machines and new buildings, there was always the possibility of a loss and the necessity of reaching a new break-even point.

To reach your first break-even point you must increase your sales while keeping your costs under control.

*In my busy and wealthy little town of Los Altos, California--and probably in your town--there are retail stores which start and vanish every month. What is obvious to the explorative pedestrian is that the public does not even know that some of these stores exists.*

*They open in small obscure passage-ways and by-ways, lie quietly for several months, do little or no business, and just as quietly close.*

*Some are in elegant new buildings, have expensive inventories, and great hopes. Occasionally we see a notice of bankruptcy taped to the locked door. Others just close. Their owners didn't know about break-even points.*

If the owners of these failing stores knew about their break-even points, they would know they had to increase their sales--and by how much.

The owners of the unknown stores would stand on the sidewalk and call out to passers-by. In fact, none paint the name of their store on the side of their private autos. They would rather have their store fail.

Failure to advertise and increase sales is not the only cause of failure. Another cause is excessive fixed costs.

The owner who rents the biggest, fanciest store or factory space in town may have started with fixed costs which exceed the possible total income. Look around your town at the little stores and think about how much they must sell just to pay one fixed cost, the rent. Apply these thoughts to your company.

The break-even graph shows something else. As your volume increases--and time goes by--the price may decrease. Competition and increased production efficiency may cause this. (Inflation is besides the point--it raises both prices and costs.)

What is important is that you have always the right price. Too high will bring you no business. Too low and you will not break even.

## The Right Price

The right price is the highest price the customer will pay without becoming forever resentful.

If the customer has an alternative, if there are other suppliers he can turn to, if you are not "holding him up," no price he pays is too high. He will not pay too much; rather, he will buy from someone else--or not buy at all. A price that isn't paid doesn't matter.

The ideal situation is the one in which you can sell for a high price because the customer likes your intangibles. He is willing to pay for quality, for service, for courtesy, for quick delivery, and for other such things which really don't cost you much. A good reputation can be worth a million dollars.

I know a company, whose name I won't tell, that had, when I worked for them, a long-standing policy on pricing competitive products:

"PRICE HIGHER THAN THE COMPETITION."

> 1999 NOTE: OK, I'll tell you who: Hewlett-Packard. Dave and Bill believed in providing a better product and better service and never getting into price competition. They could do this because of their reputation for a good product and for standing behind that product. Needless to say, they were more profitable than the competitors, could spend more money on new products, grow faster than their competitors.

Setting your prices high, and getting by with it, makes for a relaxed way of doing business. By pricing high you can be a relaxed millionaire.

Prices may be set in many ways. Here are some of the methods by which you may set yours:

1. THE GOING MARKET PRICE. This is determined by forces out of your control. You follow the lead. You may not know how the price was first determined. The economists say it was "supply and demand." They are probably wrong. Look for a way to sell at a higher price.

2. PRICE LEADERSHIP. One of the largest companies sets its prices. All other companies followed. There is no price competition. This is the way prices are set in the United States for most of the major products, such as steel, aluminum, gasoline, and automobiles.

3. ORGANIZED PRICING. Prices are set by an industry association or by a government "regulator." This is the way prices are set for utilities, railroads, and trucking. Associations of physicians, lawyers, and auto repair shops publish "standard rates" and thereby fix prices because the standard rates act as minimums.

4. CUSTOMARY FORMULA. Retail stores customarily use a mark-up of 50%, which means they sell the products for twice the cost to them. This formula is based on nothing but custom. Discount stores have been very successful with lower mark-ups. It was the abuse of the 50% formula that led to the growth of discount stores. Don't just go along with custom. Think.

5. PRICING BASED ON COSTS. Costs ultimately limit the price of all products. Pricing below costs is sometimes done to bring in customers. These bargains are "loss leaders." Prices may also be cut below the cost in order to drive competitors out of business. Corporations commonly have a division operating at a loss while the whole corporation is profitable. The competitors of that division are being subjected to prices below costs.

More often the reason for pricing below costs is that the company owner, you, doesn't know his costs.

## Know Your Costs

Many company owners have in their heads some idealized picture of how much one employee should be able to do. They also idealize their use of materials, forgetting the scrap. They fail to include overhead in their thinking. Almost all of their cost-guessing errors make them think their costs are lower than they are.

They set their price low and are delighted to beat out the competition. Their sales rise and they run out of money. Something went wrong.

Don't forget any of your costs. Keeping good books in which every payment is recorded and assigned to an account will enable you to see what your costs are. Here are some of the ways in which costs are usually classified:

1. DIRECT MATERIAL: the material that goes out the door in the finished product.

2. DIRECT LABOR: the labor that brings the direct material from the loading dock, shapes it into a product, tests it, puts it into a box, and ships it to the customer. Direct labor touches the direct material and the product.

3. OVERHEAD: the labor and material which are necessary, but not directly in the product. Rent, utilities, maintenance, depreciation, interest, and the owner's salary are examples of overhead. Keep it to a minimum.

4. PRODUCT DEVELOPMENT AND THE VARIOUS SORTS OF RESEARCH AND ENGINEERING. Because many of these costs far pre-cede the sale of the product and are not easily assigned to a particular product, they are a part of your overhead.

5. SELLING. A salesman may sell more than one product. Advertising may sell the company, not a specific product. These costs are overhead.

6. GENERAL AND ADMINISTRATIVE. The salary of accountants, lawyers, and other non-productive but essential types. Also overhead. Cut it to the bone but keep the quality.

If you are making only one product, add up all of the above costs, plus the taxes the government requires you to collect from your customers. Divide that gross cost by the number of products you are selling--or plan to sell--and get the necessary price to break-even.

If you are making more than one product, or if you want a better understanding of the costs of your product, you must separate the costs.

A typical cost breakdown of a one-product company might look like this:

|  | Total | Each |
|---|---|---|
| Direct material | $ 70,000 | $ 7.00 |
| Direct labor | 60,000 | 6.00 |
| Manuf. overhead | 26,000 | 2.60 |
| Product development | 51,000 | 5.10 |
| Selling | 20,000 | 2.00 |
| General & Admin. | 12,000 | 1.20 |
| Total cost .... | 239,000 | 23.90 |
| Profit & owner's draw | 29,000 | 2.90 |
| **Taxes** | **17,000** | **1.70** |
| Total sales and Price | $ 285,000 | $ 28.50 |

As time goes on, you will be able to use simple formulas to estimate the price you need for your products. Rather than add the costs for each product, as done above, you can use the known relationships.

For example, in the above list, the direct cost of the product is $15.00. The total costs and profit come to $28.50, which is 2.2 times the direct costs.

The price of a new product can be estimated by determining the direct costs and multiplying by 2.2.

Although costs may be known, and the price must ultimately conform to the costs, the other methods of pricing must be given weight. You may be able to price some of your products far above their costs.

Company reputation may be more important than your costs. If you have a monopoly your price can be well above your costs--whatever will sell.

## Marginal Pricing – Cardinal Sin

You may be tempted to use marginal pricing. In any plant there is some unused space. Every machine is capable of producing more--on a second shift or by more efficient operation. Every worker can produce more. So, in principle, your company can produce more with little additional cost.

This may tempt you to set a low price to sell the added product that seems to cost so little. You may think you can sell a new product at a low price because the marginal cost will be low.

If you apply such marginal costing to each new product, you will one day have all your products priced too low. Each product must bear its fair share of the total costs. Adding a product with little added costs reduces the costs of all your products, but the new product must carry its share, not just the small added cost.

DO NOT USE MARGINAL PRICING.

# Action

1. Make a Cash Forecast or review the one you have. Is your cash used efficiently? Are you going to have enough cash ?

2. Make a Break-Even Graph for your business or for a new product. What sales volume do you need to break-even?

3. Review your prices. Make sure they are high enough.

# 8 -Your Management of Wealth

**The government loves company owners**

and the managers of large corporations. This is not the place to think about the social merits of this system, both good and questionable though they may be. What you want to do is get into this system and enjoy the benefits. Let some one else worry about social philosophy.

## A Few Gifts from Uncle Sam

You can buy books that will tell you how the government will give you, the company owner, a hundred and more gifts. Here are a few of these goodies listed by one publisher:

*Deductions for your spouse's expenses...it may be a good idea to take your spouse along to help on business trips... you can probably deduct more than your half of the total cost even when your spouse is just along for personal reasons.*

*...how to set things up so you get 100% reimbursement plus an over $1,000 tax deduction as well for car expenses.*

*...two approaches to obtaining business deductions for entertaining in your home.*

*...the tax-wise way to handle such small items as taxi fares, phone calls, tips and so on.*

*How to nail down credit-card deductions.*

*...the one sure way for the top executive (you) in a close corporation to get every legitimate deduction .*

*Mixing business and pleasure...*

*here's how to add substantial sums to your total tax savings.*

*Dolling up your office?--An important Tax Court ruling has opened a great tax-saving avenue for executives (you) who take it upon themselves to add some extra class to their office decor beyond what is provided for them.*

You will be able to travel to a distant city or country, take your wife for half-price, stay in the best hotel at company expense, invite your friends to an expensive restaurant with the taxpayers paying half the bill--the company paying the other half. You want to help share the wealth and the taxes. The wealth for you. The taxes for someone else.

---

1999 NOTE: From time to time the Congress plays with the tax laws. They make them more complicated. You need to find a really competent income-tax accountant to tell you what you can and cannot do.

---

## The Redistribution of the Wealth

The federal income tax is assumed by the public to "soak the rich" by its progressive base rates. In fact, the income tax is only slightly

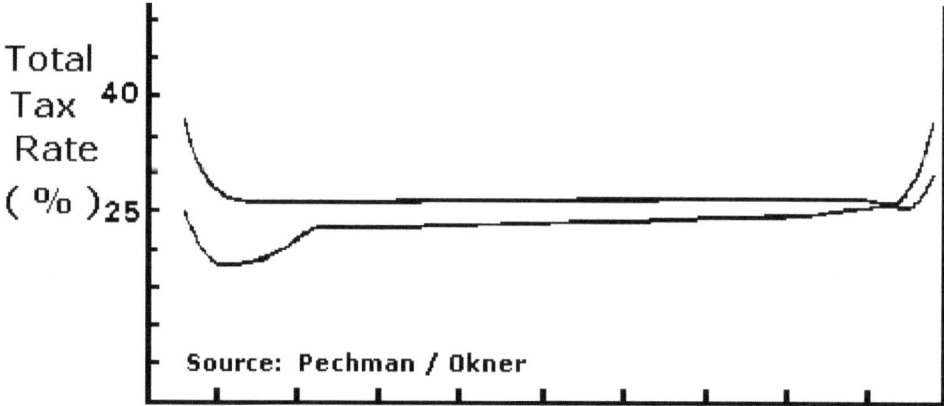

Total Tax Rate ( % )

40

25

Source: Pechman / Okner

progressive. Loopholes, called "deductions" and exemptions" and "tax shelters," all reduce the taxes paid by rich company owners, such as you. Other taxes are even more favorable for the people who have the most money.

*"The United States tax system imposes tax essentially proportional to income for the vast majority of families and therefore has little effect on the distribution of income."*

## Who Pays Taxes?

1999 NOTE: This is old data. The growth of transfer payments greatly complicates the picture. For wage- earners the picture may now be worse because of the large and regressive FICA paycheck deductions.

The graph above was the conclusion of a careful study by Joseph Pechman and Benjamin Okner of the Brookings Institute. Their study included state and local taxes as well as the federal income tax.

In our proportional tax system, almost everyone pays the same percentage of their income as taxes. When the study was made, the percentage was twenty-four. The very poor and the very rich pay slightly more.

The tax leaves the rich with income to put into savings investments. These investments, often tax-free, give them more income. This positive feedback makes the wealthy richer. The worker has much less opportunity to do this. He and she must spend most of their income for necessities. They cannot accumulate large savings to earn them more money.

You can accumulate great wealth by starting with a small business. The growth of your business will be your greatest savings and tax-free. Your savings kept in your company will earn more money, tax-free, and will pile up so high you won't know how to spend it.

Here is how you, the business owner, will get rich while your employees are getting nowhere. Which would you rather be?

| | OWNER | EMPLOYEE |
|---|---|---|
| Wages or salary | $56,000 | $12,000 |
| (less 25% taxes) | 14,000 | 3,000 |
| After tax income | 42,000 | 9,000 |
| Cost of living | 25,150 | 8,000 |
| Savings, yearly | 16,850 | 1,000 |
| Savings, 30 years | | |
| (with 5% interest) | $1,120,000 | $66,000 |
| Retirement income | | |
| (at 5% interest) | $56,000 | $ 3,300 |

And the Owner has the Company

The million dollars of savings is in addition to the value of the company and its profits. The company owner is a millionaire twice over: first by means of dollar savings and then by ownership of the company--which he can sell for $1,000,000 or more.

With less than five times the income, the company will have more than sixteen time the savings--plus the company. This accumulation of wealth can be continued by your family from generation to generation. The company owner could spend a million and still have a million. He has both high savings and the ownership of the company.

As a rich company owner, you will be able to get more interest on your savings than will your employees. Your company Treasurer will be happy to advise you.

You can buy tax-free government bonds and invest in tax shelters. Each tax shelter will be some scheme that will lose money for a year or two, then become profitable. During the losing years the losses will reduce your income tax so you won't lose half as much as it seems. Then when the tax- shelter scheme becomes profitable, you can sell it for a capital gain. The capital gain tax is much less than the income tax your employees pay.

Although you can save more money than your employees can, because you won't need all your income to live on, the government has made special provisions to help you. It has done this by making many ways in which a company owner can reduce his taxes.

These tax reductions are a form of expenditure by the government. Rather than collect the tax, then spend it as a return to certain taxpayers, the tax is simply not collected.

Such tax relief is called a "tax expenditure." These expenditures are recognized by the Congress as a way of spending. They are now tabulated in the national budget. These moneys go only to those who would otherwise have paid the highest tax--company owners such as you.

The Treasury Department has listed 57 regulations which provide such gifts to taxpayers. Of those, only ten are advantageous to workers. The workers receive only 17% of this money. The richer half--mostly company owners like you--receive 83% of the money.

---

1999 NOTE: I counted 154 tax expenditures in Table 33-4 of "The Budget for Fiscal Year 1999." The total for the five years, 1999 to 2003 is about three *trillion* dollars.

---

Think of this as taxes collected then returned to certain selected tax-payers, mostly corporations. The richest 1.2% of the people get 15% of the tax-expenditure money.

---

(1999 NOTE: that's 1980 data.)

---

To get your share you need to own a company. Regardless of the size of your company and regardless of the profit it may make, the fact that you own a company opens the door of the U.S. Treasury to you.

As a business owner, you have a right to your share of these subsidies. Owning a company is the surest way to get a capital gain. A company can own property. The government will return part of the cost of the property as tax deductions. You can depreciate your property fast. The faster your company grows, the greater will be your share of the tax subsidies.

The income tax has peculiarities not only in its treatment of the workers and owners, but also in the social values it supports. This book is not about social values. Our purpose here is to make millionaires.

The point here is that the government will penalize you as an employee and reward you handsomely as a company owner. Be an owner and take full advantage of the system.

The wealth of company owners is above and beyond what they might rightly expect from their creativity, daring, and hard work. Compare yourfself with one of your employees. Call him Charlie, your bookkeeper.

Here are some of the money transfers from workers to company owners, according to the U.S Office of Management and Budget.

---

1999 NOTE: this is 1980 data.

---

### SOME FEDERAL TAX SUBSIDIES YOU CAN USE

| | | |
|---|---:|---|
| Capital gain tax | $ 6,150,000,000 | yes |
| Home mortgage interest | 4,870,000,000 | yes |
| Home property taxes | 4,060,000,000 | yes |
| Rental housing fast depreciation | 375,000,000 | perhaps |
| Life insurance interest | 1,420,000,000 | perhaps |
| Charitable contributions | 3,820,000,000 | probably |
| Tax-free state & local bonds | 1,060,000,000 | probably |
| Farming expense & capital gain | 1,100,000,000 | perhaps |
| Imputed net rent, owner | 500,000,000 | perhaps |
| Untaxed capital gains at death | 700,000,000 | probably |
| Dividend exclusion | 320,000,000 | yes |
| Investment credit | 880,000,000 | yes |
| Excess depletion | 305,000,000 | perhaps |
| Excess depreciation | 220,000,000 | yes |
| Personal total . . . . . . . . . . . . . | $ 28,300,000,000 | |
| Corporation subsidies . . . . . . . . | $20,260,000,000 | yes |
| Total subsidy . . . . . . . . . . . . . . | $ 48,560,000,000 | |

### Poor Charlie: Your Bookkeeper

1999 NOTE:
This section, as was this book, was written in 1980. The tax laws have changed, notably by the 1986 reforms under Reagan. Some of the details have changed, not the general situation of poor Charlie

Charlie earns $15,000. It is taxed. Your son can receive $15,000 income from a trust fund you set up. The trust fund will be invested in tax- free bonds. Your son need pay no income tax. Money earned by Charlie's labor is taxed. Money earned by the clever investment of money earned by someone else is not taxed.

Charlie earned $1,000 on a part-time night job. His extra money will be taxed (unless he can arrange to be paid in currency, not reported, and risks the penalty for tax evasion). You can receive $1,000 in gifts from you best supplier friends. Gifts are not taxed. Only work is fully taxed.

Charlie keeps his savings in a bank, they pay him 5^% interest, which is less than the rate of inflation. Charlie is losing his savings. This is a form of taxation we'll come back to later in this chapter. You can avoid this tax by keeping your savings in your company.

You, the company owner, keep your cash savings in "money-market" certificates or funds, municipal bonds that are tax-free, and other places that pay interest equal to the rate of inflation. But most of your savings are safely in your company.

In his spare time, Charlie writes a book on book-keeping. When he sells it he will pay income tax on what he gets. If in your company an invention is made and patented, perhaps by one of your employees, you can sell the patent and pay only a capital gain tax. On the same income, your tax will be much less than Charlie's.

Charlie takes night classes to learn to be a paramedic. He wants to help humanity. He cannot deduct the cost of the school to reduce his tax. You can take all the classes in money- making, business management, and investment that you wish. You can deduct the cost because the class is related to your business. Almost anything is. You get your school for half of what Charlie must pay.

Poor Charlie gets hit by a tornado and the medical bills come to $1,400. Only $990 will be deductible and that only reduces his tax by $250. The accident costs Charlie $1,150.

The same tornado wrecks your car. Your loss is also $1,400 (dents in your Mercedes). Your loss is all deductible. The U.S. Congress rates property more important than people.

## Share Your Wealth Equally and Have More

Entrepreneurs such as yourself, the keystones of free enterprise, are the greatest beneficiaries of that system of economic government. They can and do become millionaires and billionaires. It might be expected that they would pay their "fair share" of the taxes and also share the wealth with their employees.

We have seen that there may be some doubts about the sharing of the taxes. Let's next look at the sharing of the wealth after taxes.

An instructive example of free-enterprise at its best is the Hewlett-Packard corporation. Because the company has grown from two people to a giant with little of the confusion of mergers, corporate buyouts, and the like, the records are clear and available to us.

Starting in a very small garage with one drill press and a great deal of ability. Bill Hewlett and Dave Packard built their two-billion dollar company with more than 50,000 employees and still growing. Their company facilitated the electronic industry of the United States and of the world. Their instruments are in every laboratory and engineering room. For this there was a profit.

Hewlett-Packard was incorporated in 1947 for tax advantages and for the limitation of liability. All the shares belonged to the founders. This was the first money printed by the company. By 1980, the company had issued 59 million shares and the market value of those shares was more than $5.4 billion.

The company never sold shares to the public at large. It did not "go public" directly. Of this I was informed by the Treasurer of Hewlett-Packard in 1980. Shares were sold to key employees by way of stock options and to all other employees through stock-purchase plans. Such shares were sold at a discount from the market price.

The employees and the founders sold shares to the public from time to time. Both the employees and the public, as well as the founders, benefitted from the growing value of the company.

Most of the company's capital came from earnings retained (positive feedback). As of October 31, 1979, the company had raised only 26% of its capital by selling 59 million shares for $326 million, mostly to employees. (Some shares were traded for other companies acquired.)

Therefore all the share owners together had gained a total of $3,074 million. This was over many years and many trades of shares among employees and the public.

The employees received a total pay-roll of nearly three billion dollars from the start of the company in 1939 until 1980. This can be computed from occasional reports of the number of employees and the payroll.

The share holders (owners) of Hewlett-Packard have gained about three billion dollars. The employees gained wages of about three billion dollars. This is the formula between owner's gain and employees' wages:

## Equal Sharing

The owner's wealth is equal to the sum of all wages paid to employees since the founding of the company.

If you own the whole company, you will gain as much wealth as the total wages of all your employees over the life of your company. The sharing is equal.

If there are many shareholders, they necessarily divide up the owner's gain. For the greatest wealth, let your company grow slowly if necessary but keep the whole thing for yourself.

You do not need to incorporate your company and sell shares. As the case of Hewlett-Packard illustrates, the money you get by selling shares can be and probably should be a minor and unnecessary part of your financing. The main purposes of incorporation are to avoid taxes and to give shares to your key employees.

Your employees can be given a more equal share. There is nothing to prevent this except greed on the part of the company owner. For many years the San Francisco attorney, Louis Kelso, has advocated a distribution of ownership to employees. We mentioned his books in Chapter 1.

Kelso proposes that the workers be given shares in the companies for which they work. Such plans have been offered in a minor way by some corporations. They sell their shares to employees at a discount. Several "Kelso plans" have been formulated, called Employee Stock Ownership Plans (ESOP's) and Employee Stock Ownership Trusts (ESOT's). More common are less formal plans for employees to buy stock at a small discount if they wish to.

You should be aware of the possibility that such a plans might be used to unload a failing corporation on unwitting employees.

Nothing prevents the owner from sharing fairly with his employees. At present, employees are not aware of the inequality of the prevalent sharing formula.

Now that you know how valuable your employees are, you will give them a bigger share.

You can still make your company grow by reinvesting the employee's surplus production. If you give shares in the company to your employees, the money stays in the company. In other words, you are printing your own "company" money which costs you nothing. But your employees can gain if your company grows. They'll work harder to make it grow if they have a share.

The distorted system of distributing the wealth is largely due to the ways in which the governments collect taxes. You and your company are parties to that system.

## Your Company as a Tax Collector

The notion that a corporation is a person, a person who pays taxes, is a commonly held belief. Don't be a dummy.

A century of propaganda and legal mumbo-jumbo has taught us that the corporations are persons who have Constitutional rights. More than anything else, this novel notion has led us all to think of corporations as people. They are not people and certainly not freed black slaves. But it is a fact that the status of corporations, which you should take advantage of, has derived from a Constitutional amendment which makes no mention of corporations.

The 14th amendment was intended to give equal rights to the freed black slaves. It was not used for that purpose for one-hundred years. In the meantime, the corporations were given equal rights with persons. They were declared by the Supreme Court to be persons under the 14th amendment. "Persons" is the word used in that amendment. Few who voted for the amendment thought it meant corporations.

Persons though they are, corporations cannot pay taxes. They have no magic source of money, no hidden treasure, from which to pay taxes. Only workers have such a source: their labor.

Real people do have a source of magic money with which to pay taxes. They draw money from their earnings that would otherwise have been spent for food, clothing, housing, and fun. Taxes are paid only by individual, real people who shift their consumption from private things to government things.

The shift is enforced by the collection of taxes. Retail stores collect "sales" taxes in a direct way. Corporations also collect taxes on sales, but this tax is not identified as the sales tax that it really is. They add to their prices amounts equal to what they pay in income and other taxes.

There is a "sales tax" – name it what you will -- of approximately two-percent attributable to the income tax on businesses. As tax collectors, corporations set their prices up by two percent to get money to pay the tax. This is recorded on conventional financial statements as a part of "gross sales." When we trace this amount down the Earnings Statements we find that it accounts for half of their before-tax reported profit. (You know that true profit is much greater.) Then they pay that half of their profit as income tax--just what they collected.

In round numbers, lumping all governments, this is a dimly-lit picture of the national total profit and tax statement:

| | |
|---|---:|
| SALES | $ 3,000,000,000,000 |
| "SALES TAX" COLLECTED | 60,000,000,000 |
| SALES REPORTED | 3,060,000,000,000 |
| ALL COSTS | -2,940,000,000,000 |
| PROFIT REPORTED | 120,000,000,000 |
| "INCOME TAX" PAID | - 60,000,000,000 |
| AFTER-TAX PROFIT | $ 60,000,000,000 |

As a company-owner, you are a tax-collector. You must get the money to pay the taxes. Don't pay them yourself. Set your prices to cover the tax just as you cover all other costs. Taxes are a cost of doing business and must be paid by your customers.

Here are some of the taxes you, as a business owner, must collect:
COLLECT, Not "pay" – <u>collect</u>:

*Federal income tax*

*State income taxes*

*Local payroll taxes*

*Social Security taxes*

*Federal unemployment insurance*

*State unemployment and disability*

*Sales tax*

*Property tax*

Don't be misled by the fact that some of these may be called "employer contributions." The source of money for one is the same as for all. Your customers supply the tax money. Your employees supply your wealth but that's in the true profit, not in the reported profit.

Congressmen would have you think that the corporation income tax is paid by wealthy shareholders by way of reduced dividends. This is not so. Dividends are set to a level that will give the shares a reasonable value. A change in the tax paid would not affect the dividends. Competition would compel a change in prices. It is the customers who pay taxes. You, the company owner, are the collector. Note also that many corporations do not pay dividends. How then can income tax be a reduction of dividends? Owners benefit by company growth, not by profit, i.e. dividends.

## The Theft of Your Savings

Taxes shouldn't bother you. You don't have to pay them. But there is another way the government may get your money. It can take your savings.

Here are some of the ways in which you can hold your savings:

| Dollar-valued | Property-valued |
|---|---|
| *lost to inflation* | *inflation-proof* |
| *Currency* | *Your home* |
| *Checking accounts* | *Real estate* |
| *Savings accounts* | *Personal property* |
| *Bonds* | *Skills* |
| *Savings bonds* | *Company money* |
| *Life insurance* | *Food in storage* |
| *Social Security Fund* | *Precious metal* |

The property-valued items have value no matter what happens to the dollar. Their market value may fluctuate but their intrinsic value--their usefulness--remains after the dollars become worthless.

The total dollar-valued savings in the United States in 1977 was

$ 1,895,000,000,000 – almost two trillion (not B illion)

That year the consumer price index rose by 6.9 percent. Multiplying, we find that the people who held their savings in dollar form lost  $ 122,000,000,000. That's 122 billion dollars lost in one year.

The inflation rate in 1979 was close to 12 percent and the loss of savings must exceed $ 250,000,000,000.

This money lost to savers was spent by the government. The government sold bonds to raise money for current expenses--something no sane company manager would ever do. The banks bought the bonds then created money by making loans. With more money in print, the prices went up.

As the dollar lost 25% of its value from 1972 to 1976, the richest one-percent of the people increased their hold on the nation's wealth from 26.6% to 27.5%. This increase amounted to $30.4 billion transferred from 99% of the people to the richest one percent.

You, as a business owner, can be on the receiving end of this massive transfer of the nation's wealth from employees to owners.

We have seen, in the story of Charlie your bookkeeper, how your employees get lower interest on their savings. They also lose because their income does not keep up with inflation.

Economists have a saying: "Wages go up the stairway. Prices take the elevator." Only a few percent of the workers, those belonging to aggressive unions, manage to keep up with inflation.

To you the owner of a company of employees this means that your workers generally take a cut in real wages because of inflation. You can keep your prices even with inflation.


Inflation can make you richer because much of your wealth is not in dollars but in hard assets and employees..


Between 1946 and 1976 the people of the United States who did not own a business LOST MORE THAN $800 BILLION OF THEIR SAVINGS BY INFLATION. During those years the federal deficit rose by $620" billion and the state and local governments accounted for the rest.

All governments have done this for the last 4,000 years. Plan on it.

The graph on the next page shows how savings have been stolen since 1947.

Dollar-valued savings lost half their value in twenty six years from 1947 to 1975.

Dollar-valued savings lost half their value in eleven years from 1967 to 1978.

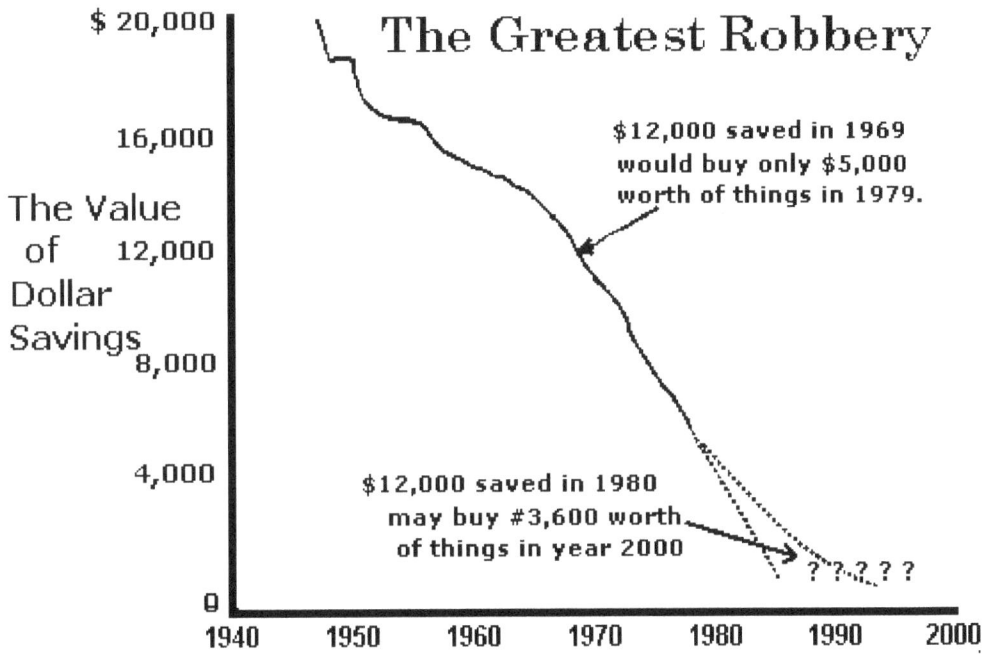

**The Greatest Robbery**

$12,000 saved in 1969 would buy only $5,000 worth of things in 1979.

$12,000 saved in 1980 may buy #3,600 worth of things in year 2000

# Action

1. In the table below, find the REAL VALUE of your savings at the age of 65. The table shows what you'll be able to buy with your savings if you save $1,000 each year at 6 % interest with various rates of inflation.

| Your present age | What you'll be able to buy at age 65 if this is the average inflation rate | | | | | What you put in the bank |
|---|---|---|---|---|---|---|
| | 4% | 6% | 8% | 10% | 13% | |
| 20 | $ 39,000 | 16,000 | 7,000 | 3,000 | 1,000 | $ 45,000 |
| 25 | 34,000 | 16,000 | 7,000 | 4,000 | 1,000 | 40,000 |
| 30 | 30,000 | 15,000 | 8,000 | 4,000 | 2,000 | 35,000 |
| 35 | 26,000 | 15,000 | 8,000 | 5,000 | 2,000 | 30,000 |
| 40 | 22,000 | 14,000 | 9,000 | 5,000 | 3,000 | 25,000 |
| 45 | 18,000 | 12,000 | 8,000 | 6,000 | 4,000 | 20,000 |
| 50 | 14,000 | 10,000 | 8,000 | 6,000 | 4,000 | 15,000 |
| 55 | 9,000 | 8,000 | 7,000 | 5,000 | 4,000 | 10,000 |

2. Notice that even with an inflation rate of 4% less than the assumed interest rate you will end up with less real value in your savings than the dollars you put in the bank. Take action now to get your savings into your own business, where it can grow and be safe from inflation.

---

2015 :NOTE: The rates used above look strange in 2015 when inflation is about one percent. (it will go up). But the story is unchanged. Inflation destroys dollar savings.

---

# 9 – How to Make Yourself a Winner

You want to be a millionaire. You now own a company. You have company money, but you must make it valuable.

You know how owning a company can make you rich. You are examining product ideas--perhaps you are already in business.

But, are you a winner? Do you feel sure that you will succeed? Are you afraid to start? Are you afraid to expand your business? Fear is the reason there are only 520,000 millionaires in the United States. Every man who has a job could become a millionaire if he could overcome fear.

Are you a future millionaire? Can you start your company and make it grow? Do you know how to adjust your- self to become a winner? You are not the first future millionaire to have doubts. There are things you can do about your doubts.

## The Enterprising Man

Henry David Thoreau said: "The mass of men lead lives of quiet desperation." He may have exaggerated, or he may have had in mind the men who become entrepreneurs.

A study of entrepreneurs was made by Michigan State University researchers. They learned these things about the enterprising man:

"The typical entrepreneur differs from the big-business executive in that he cannot live within a frame-work of occupational behavior set by others.

"From his early work experiences, the entrepreneur slowly fashions his conception of how skills, money, equipment, and markets can be brought into a profitable combination. Many had left school at an early age and did so because of a feeling of restlessness, of 'not getting anywhere.' Another point was the place of adult figures, more than any other one factor, sets him apart from the men who spend their lives in large organizations and who accept directives handed down by 'leaders.'

"The act of entrepreneurship is that of bringing skills, money, equipment, and markets together into a profitable combination. From his early work experiences, the entrepreneur slowly fashions his conception of how this can be done.

"Eventually, the typical entrepreneur finds the pattern of his life disrupted. There is a sudden or progressive loss of economic security, a loss of goals and aspirations that have guided him. But it is not the fact of the disruption of his life that sets him apart as an entrepreneur. It is that, during this time, there occurred to him: <u>the possibility of establishing a business of his own</u>." Has it occurred to you?

Has it occurred to you that there is a possibility of establishing a business of your own? American millionaires are enterprising men--except for those who limit themselves to being the sons and grandsons of enterprising men. Some millionaires knew the method of using the system and knew the source of wealth. Most did not know these when they started. None talk about them.

Some millionaires started companies only to earn a living and accidentally became wealthy. It is typical of millionaires to say, *"I just wanted to make a living. I had no idea that I would get rich."*

They did not know that they were using a method or gathering about them a Secret Source of wealth. You will have the advantage of knowing the system from the start.

You have title to a company. Almost all American millionaires got their start by owning a company. No matter what the method used to make money, owning a company to do it is the surest way to get rich.

Any man who has ideas and can make decisions needs helpers to use those ideas and carry out those decisions. The man who gets help is an ENTREPRENEUR. Men or women who do it by themselves are ECCENTRICS. The man or woman who works for another is lazy, ignorant, or simply a casual person who prefers to have someone else make the decisions. And what is bad is that the employed worker is the one who takes the risks.

Nothing is more dangerous than to be an employee. Five out of six employees who live to be 65 will be unable to support themselves in old age on their savings alone. To say nothing of the continual risk of losing a job. Workers think they are playing it safe by working for a pension and not taking the imagined risks of starting their own companies. It is they, the workers, who take the greatest risk.

The fact that you are reading this tells us that you don't want to take the great risk of being a worker. You want to be an employer--to own your own business. You want to know the American Millionaire's Method and his Secret Source of wealth. You are an ENTERPRISING PERSON.

You are not alone. The number of millionaires in the United States is growing more and more rapidly. The enormous variety and growth of our industry provides more and more opportunities to become wealthy. There is room for more millionaires, including you, if you are a winner.

## Are You a Winner?

Winners and losers were studied by Dr. Jack J. Hayden. What he learned will help you both to start and to manage your growing company.

Dr. Hayden was led to make his study by his observations of winners and losers on the stock market. He saw that:

*"In speculative markets the emotions are nearly all that count. Intellectualism has little meaning there, for the markets are primordial jungles requiring elemental survival characteristics."*

You should stay out of the stock and commodity markets until after you have made your million dollars, then the loss of a hundred-thousand dollars now and then won't matter much.

What Dr. Hayden shows us is that people can be classified in two ways:

Optimists / Pessimists

and

Risk-Takers / Risk-Avoiders

An optimist may be fearful of taking risk. He may believe that all is right with the world, but fear that his own product or company idea may fail.

The pessimist may be certain the world is going to collapse, but have no fear that his own plans will fail.

On the chart below you will see the four extreme cases in the corners--and room for all degrees between them.

```
No Fear | Lacks hope              Takes unnecessary
of Risk | for future             and risky choices

   ↑              Millionaire
   |            Business Owners
 Risk                HERE
Avoidance

   ↑
   |
   |
Terrified | Can do     There are no     Acts, but is
by Risk   | nothing    entrepeneurs       always
                       down here          too late

         Pessimist ─────────────→  Optimist
```

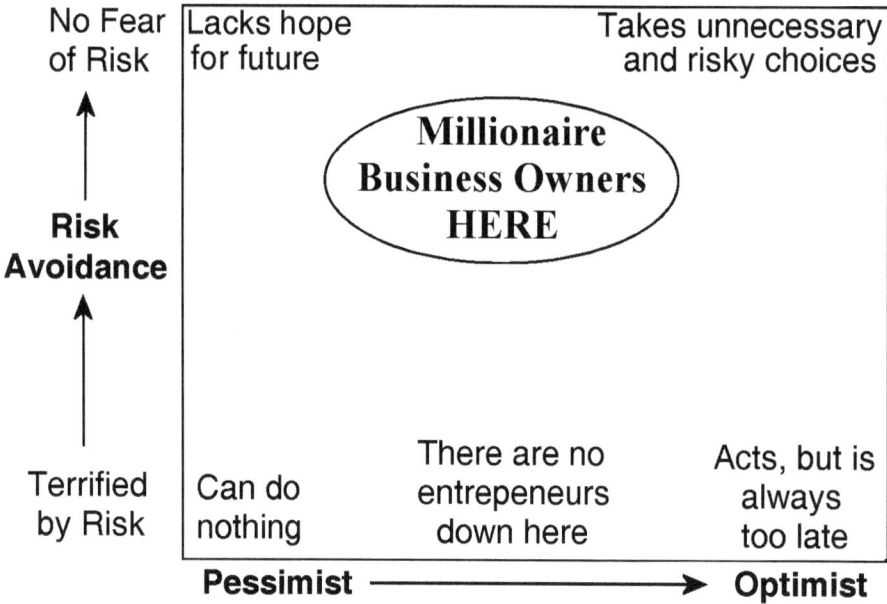

The four "corner" cases are these:

Fearless Optimist: tries anything; takes too much risk

Frightened Optimist: acts too late.

Fearless Pessimist: acts quickly; but too conservatively.

Timid Pessimist: can do nothing.

You should locate yourself on this chart. Here's how.

If you think the business climate is not right to start a company, you are pessimistic. The business climate has absolutely nothing to do with the starting time for a new company. A new company offers something new. Whether there is a depression, or a recession, or a business boom, the new company can start.

The new company owner doesn't expect, doesn't need, and can't deliver the big sales you may mentally associate with times of prosperity. Your company can more easily hire good employees the source of wealth--during recessions. By the time prosperity comes back, your company will be prepared to take advantage of the bigger spending.

Re: Time now for class-action to protect $$MM investments in XPIf you think the dollar is always going to have value and that your savings account is safe, you are wildly optimistic. If you think any company you start will succeed, no matter how badly you manage it, you are an optimist. In a moment, I will tell you how to adjust yourself to the best balance of optimism/pessimism. But right now, decide where you now then fit on this scale.

On the risk-avoidance scale, Dr. Hayden found that people could be positioned by the amount of information they needed to reach a decision. The high risk-avoiders need repeated information--redundancy--before they can make a decision. Those who are low in risk-avoidance can act on the first good piece of information. They strike "while the iron is hot." Those high in risk-avoidance are always too late. By the time they act, the situation has changed and the information is about to reverse--much to their dismay.

In the stock market, the high risk-avoidance people buy when the market is high and everyone is optimistic. They sell when the market is at a bottom and everybody is gloomy. As entrepreneurs, they always get in on the dying tail-end of fads.

Can you act on the basis of the first good information? Or must you hear the story confirmed many times before you act? Are you afraid to change jobs when you hear of a better job, then feel disappointed when someone grabs the job? Are you afraid to buy something because the price is too high--then disappointed when the price goes still higher? How much information do you need before you act?

This book is a good test of your risk avoidance. Here you have been repeatedly shown that you can become wealthy by going into a business in which you have employees to produce your wealth. Every day you see this system working in the businesses in your town. Who are the wealthiest people in your town? They have employees. You now have the information. How many repetitions does it take before you act?

Some people act and get rich, while others only dream. The rich people were low in risk-avoidance and had a good balance of optimism and pessimism. You can be the same.


WHO ARE YOU?  FEARLESS?  RISK-AVOIDER?
OPTIMIST?  PESSIMIST?

Now pause in your reading and place yourself on the chart. Be honest with yourself. Nobody is watching. If you are fair about it, you need take no costly psychological tests to learn if you can be a successful company owner.

Place yourself first with regards to your feelings about the future of your business. This is the optimism/ pessimism scale. Then place yourself on the scale of risk-avoidance. You know yourself.

The exercise of locating yourself on this chart will help you make the adjustments that may be needed. To be a winner, to start a company and to manage its growth well, you must be TOP and CENTER on the chart.

You must have little fear of risk, that is to say, you must be able to act on the first good information, not wait to be told over and over again.

You must have a balance of optimism and pessimism. You cannot be ignorant of the dangers and you cannot be overwhelmed by them. You must be able to use your opportunities. You can, but you may have to make some adjustments.

## How to Make Yourself a Winner

You can change your position on the chart, both as to optimism/pessimism and as to risk-avoidance. You can manage your company so that you have little risk to fear. You can become better informed so as not to be extreme in either optimism or pessimism.

On the scale of optimism/pessimism you must be neutral. Excesses on this scale lead to bad decisions. What keeps people off center on this scale is an excess of bad news or a lack of knowledge of the world.

There are, in fact, disasters waiting for us to turn the page of the calendar. There always have been. Some people are too aware of these dangers. They are storing dry foods and gold bars in anticipation of the day of doom.

The optimists see a great future in the dry-food and gold-bar businesses.

Excessive optimism is the result of ignorance. No one in the United States today who is aware* of the realities of the operation of our economic system can be optimistic about the world economy. In spite of this, you can be optimistic about your own economic system.

You should become informed so as to cure yourself of excessive optimism. This doesn't mean you should become a pessimist. The fact is that, in the worst of all possible futures, there will be Americans getting rich. Pessimism about your future possibilities is not justified. (Unless you sit on your duff in a job, with your dollars in a savings account or in government bonds.)

Excessive pessimism is easy to get from the daily newspapers and TV. Their business is disasters past, present, and future.

Seek out the good news to balance the bad. Reduce your exposure to "gloom and doom." Balance yourself on the scale of optimism/pessimism. Balance will make you wealthy.

By using the methods of making your company safe that are described in the next chapter, you can remove the fear obstacle. You will have little or no risk to hold you back. This is one way to reduce your risk-avoidance tendency--remove the risk.

If you know how to start and run a business with patience, with safe financing methods, and with safe operating methods, you will be able to proceed as though you have no fear of risk.

# Action

1. Locate yourself on the chart of optimists/pessimists and risk avoidance. Be honest with yourself.


2. Take action to adjust your sources of information so as to be neutral on optimism/pessimism. Make yourself a realist and well informed. Ignore the prophets of gloom and doom--they're making money at it.


3. Design the operation of your business so that you can make your company grow while keeping the risk acceptable to you. Use the methods described in the next chapter.

# 10 – Risk-Free Business Ownership

You own a company. You know who has the money. You know how the government will help you with tax advantages. You know that, until you get your company moving, the government will be taking your income with taxes and your savings with inflation.

You have a product in mind, or you have already started a business. You know that the millionaire's Secret Source of wealth is employees. You know how positive feedback, the re-investment of the employees' extra production, will make your company grow.

But perhaps you are still afraid of taking risks and making decisions that might get you into financial trouble. Such fear is healthy and understandable. There is a way to get around such fear. This chapter and the next will show how a business can be run so that you will have nothing to fear.

## Failures Are Planned

The owner of a million-dollar company was asked to appraise a new company. My friend visited the company, talked to the owners, saw the plant. He found a new company which had not yet shipped its first product, but had this fine organization:

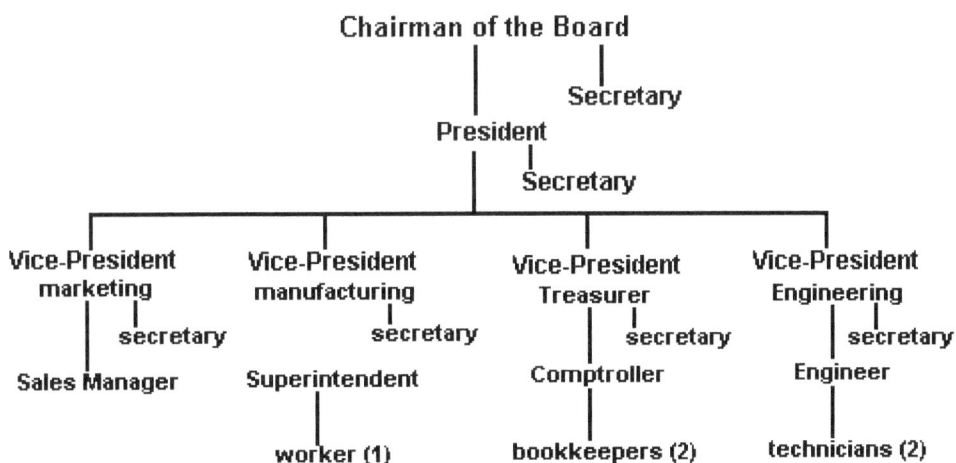

```
                    Chairman of the Board
                          |
                          |        Secretary
                          |           |
                       President
                          |
                       Secretary
          _____|_____
         |               |              |              |
Vice-President   Vice-President   Vice-President   Vice-President
  marketing       manufacturing     Treasurer        Engineering
      |                |                |                |
   secretary        secretary        secretary        secretary
      |                |                |                |
Sales Manager     Superintendent    Comptroller        Engineer
                       |                |                |
                    worker (1)     bookkeepers (2)   technicians (2)
```

My friend suggested that the company be shut down, but that it might be possible to start a new company: starting with only the engineer and the product idea. The organization was that of a multi-million dollar grand plan. The funding was that of a mom-and-pop grocery.

The money used to start a mom-and-pop grocery can start a million-dollar business. But the money must fit the organization and the organization must fit the money.

There will be no Vice-Presidents in your small company until after you've made your first $1,000,000. You don't need a Treasurer until after the money starts piling up too high to count.

What you need is workers: the makers of products and the doers of services. Then you need more workers, some of whom can be supervisors of others.

When the orders are coming in fast, you will need a clerk-typist-bookkeeper to handle the paper: the orders, the invoices, the payroll.

You will have to do the selling at first. This follows naturally from the fact that you have chosen the product. You know who the customers are and why they should buy your product. You will soon need sales representatives. They work on commission so they cost you nothing unless they make sales. Later you will need to hire a full-time salesman who can become your sales manager.

As the money starts flowing freely, you must get a part-time accountant. Find a retired CPA or former treasurer of a big company who wants to have a little fun helping a small company.

One day your company will get its first Vice-President. But that will be long after you've set this book aside and bought your summer home on a lake in Canada and your winter home in Hawaii. Then you can promote one of your employees to manage your company.

*When Mike McNeely started Applied Materials, he first hired technicians who could build his product. He did not need managers or secretaries or accountants. There was nothing to manage, no letters to type, and no money to count. He made two sales (one to me) and hired technicians to build the machines he had sold. Because his technicians were good, the machines worked, and I placed an order for a second and larger machine.*

*Within a year his company needed a comptroller to count the money. His employees were making him wealthy. Employees that make and sell the product are the key. McNeely's company was valued at $27,000,000 recently and had not yet paid a dividend--but it has lots of employees, the source of wealth.*

---

1999 NOTE: McNeely has long since gone on to start other companies. Applied Materials is the largest maker of semiconductor equipment, with sales of $1.45 billions expected next quarter. Net income for the quarter ended last week was $244.1" million. Incidentally, they sell about as much to Taiwan as to North America. From looking at their annual report it seems they don't pay dividends. This is good management of a growth company -- reinvest everything you can get your hands on. The owner's wealth is not increased by profits, but by the growth of the company.

---

In the following paragraphs, some examples of methods of operation are described which will reduce your risk. From these examples you will learn the principles. You can invent more examples as you develop your million-dollar company. The principles are found in these choices you will make.

RENT OR BUY

Most of the things you need for the operation of your company can either be rented or bought. You can lease a building or buy it. You can buy equipment, but much equipment can be leased. You may be able to find a leasing company that will buy equipment to your specification, then lease it to you. The point is, you have rent-or-buy choices to make. Which gives you the least risk?

You know that you must keep your company out of financial trouble by always having control of your cash. Things you buy cannot readily be converted back into cash. If you rent equipment on short-term contracts, you can return them and stop the flow of cash. Rental has two advantages. You need less cash and you can cut your costs quickly if you need to.

Buying has the advantage that the total cost may be less in the long run. This is particularly true during times of high inflation. You can buy at the present price and use it later when the price is higher. You may get the use of a $6,000 machine in 1988 by buying the machine for $5,000 in 1980.

If you have high profits (a mistake), buying equipment or a building may be the most efficient use of that money. In effect, what you are doing is keeping the profits of the renter for yourself.

Renting or leasing is safer than buying. Choices like this must be made every day in the management of your company. By recognizing these choices as problems of cash control, you can get rich safely.


USED OR NEW


Rather than renting to be safe, you can buy used equipment. Then, if necessary, you can sell that equipment for little less, or possibly more, than you paid for it. Consider a popular example.

Franchisers and "non-franchisers" are urging people to open quick-print shops. They make their money by selling a shop full of new equipment. A vast array of used printing equipment is on the market, much of it guaranteed.

You can rent or buy either new or used printing equipment and floor space. The franchise seller wants you to rent the floor space, either used or new, and buy his new equipment. Whether the space is used or new may not be important, but new equipment may be costly and unsafe for your cash.

New equipment, like new cars, loses much of its market value at the moment of purchase. Not only is the cost greater than for used equipment, but the loss if you have to sell is much greater. You want to run your company with little or no financial risk. If you buy good, guaranteed, used equipment and your company goes out of business, you can sell the equipment for almost as much as you paid. If you buy new equipment, you would have to sell it as used for a much lower price.

On the other hand, you may be safer to buy a building rather than rent space. A building depreciates slowly, if at all. The market value may be higher in the future than it is today. If you are going to put $40,000 into a print shop, buying a little old building and guaranteed used equipment is probably the safest way to start. Or start in your garage with some used equipment.

Used equipment, when available, conserves your cash when you buy it and returns your cash when you sell it. Used is safer. You don't plan to shut down your company, and you won't need to if you learn from this book, but you want to feel safe. <u>Feeling</u> <u>safe</u> will help you go ahead and expand your company.

Printing equipment is only one example. There are dealers in used equipment of many kinds all around the country. They will recondition and guarantee the equipment. Many kinds of equipment can be purchased used. Used store fixtures, machinery, trucks, furniture, typewriters, and buildings can be found. They are safer than new.

*Bob Denman, my friend with a million-dollar company, goes to any machinery auction he learns about. His excellent shop has been built largely with used equipment. His company has never been in danger although it is in an industry that swings from boom to bust and back. He buys used equipment and hires used (experienced) workers. Now that he has many employees as a source of money, he can spend more for used equipment, new equipment, executive cars, and a company airplane.*

> 1999 NOTE: Bob has turned over management of the company to one of his employees. The airplane was sold long ago, having outlived its usefulness. I'm tempted to tell you the company's internet web site, but won't. Bob has a right to some privacy and you're not in the market for semiconductor equipment. Suffice it to say that they are the leading company in their specialty. – and much has happened since 1999 !

A human variation of the rent-buy, new-old decision is apparent in your choice of employees. You can rent <u>people</u>. They will be temporary employees. There are agencies who stock such people. By renting people, you can run your business without the book-keeping of severance pay, pensions, unemployment insurance, and the like. The rental agency takes care of such matters, if necessary. If you rent workers, you can cut your costs quickly without firing an employee. The temporary employees know they do not have a permanent job.

Besides rent-buy, there is a new-used people decision. You can hire inexperienced (new) people and train them. You risk losing your investment in their training if you have to risk the investment of time (money) in training them. Used people, like other used equipment, are safer.

Finally, you can rent used people. That is to say, get experienced people from a temporary help agency. The Kelly Girl secretary is an example of rented, used people. Typists and machine operators and baby-sitters are common examples of rented, used people. Renting-used is safer than buying-new.

> 1999 NOTE: renting employees – "temps"--has become a big business, as has the use of part-time employees. Tax reasons..

## ONE PRODUCT OR MANY

The one-product company is like a plane with one engine. If anything goes wrong with that one vital part, the result is catastrophic. But many safe planes have only one engineer and a very reliable engine.

If you have a product which you are sure is safe, don't divert your attention from it by being in haste to diversify for safety. If you have a patent, if you have a big lead in product recognition, if your product has many uses (not really a single product), then you may be safe with one product. But even the owners of Scotch tape. Vaseline, Thermos bottles, and Band-Aids have competition.

The one-product safe company is at the mercy of the ego of the owner. Too many owners are sure that their product can never by replaced or that no one can ever make it cheaper or better. One day they are proven wrong and their company shrinks.

The trick is never to develop such an ego. That is hard for you egotistical millionaires to do. You know you are superior to people. But try. Perhaps your product needs to be up-dated. Perhaps its life is limited. Perhaps you would have less risk if you added a new product.

## IN LINE OR OUT-OF-LINE

You may expand your start a new business, your company and your you can go into a new business, or in line with past career or field.

Unless your past was in an obsolescent business, you are safer to stay "in line." By staying in the same line of business, your experience will continue to grow in a cumulative way.

Your company of employees, like yourself, is a certain set of talents and experience. In addition, your company has certain equipment and space.

These are suited to a variety of closely-related products. A machine- shop can produce some kinds of things. A bakery can produce a different kind of things. Each is versatile but neither can compete with the other.

Unfortunately, many company owners find themselves in one business, wishing they were in a different business. They try to use their company to satisfy their wish. Because their company is not capable in the new business, they are soon in trouble. What they lack is continuity.

Staying in the same line of product or service gives your company continuity. Continuity is safer. The only danger in product planning for that continuity is that you may not know what your product is.

Products are often not what they seem. What you are making and selling may be only a tool for delivering a service. An example is a computer. Computers are not the product they seem to be.

Computer manufacturers succeed or fail, not because of the quality of the hardware they make, but because of the software service and maintenance they provide. The hardware is shipped in boxes. The software is carried in briefcases and brains. A computer manufacturer does not sell computers. He sells a service: reliable computation. Know what your product is.


MANAGE OR WITHDRAW


The owner may manage his company, or hire a manager and withdraw from the "battlefield." The owner who manages has immediate knowledge of the state of his company. The owner who hires a manager and then withdraws may not know what is going on in his own company. It is safer to be your own manager.

*I worked as a middle-level manager in a $20 million company whose president tried to hire managers and with-draw. He spent his time in a remote office, never ventured into the factory, didn't know what was going on, and lost his company. (2015 note: PSI)*

*I also worked as a middle-level manager in a $120 million company whose president managed. He now has a two-billion dollar company. All of his employees knew he was "around." Everybody worked and everybody was prepared to explain what they were doing. Everybody was happy because they knew they were part of a company whose owner "cared" and managed.*

1999 NOTE: Dave is gone now
but Hewlett-Packard has sales of $50 billion.

The trick is to hire assistants, but only as fast as they are needed. Call them assistant managers, directors, or vice-presidents (titles are cheap) but never stop doing the managing, directing, or presidenting that is necessary.

Let your assistants know what is to be done. Let them do what they can. Don't hide in a remote office. The captain of a safe ship does not hide below decks, especially in a storm.

ONE MAN OR MANY MEN

One man can get sick. One man can be lacking one vital skill. There is danger is a one-man company. There is also danger in a company of many people, if one person is indispensable. No company should long allow itself to be dependent upon any one person.

There is security in numbers. Hire and train so that your company can run well, even though someone is missing. Every manager should have a replacement in training.

You are no exception. You must be replaceable too. Find among your employees someone who can someday do your job. Then you can withdraw, slowly at first, then as you wish. With your $1,000,000 to spend, you may want to get away from it all and have some fun. Perhaps you will want to start another company.

THE RETAIL-STORE RISK

To become a millionaire in retail, you must have either a very large store, a chain of stores, or a chain of franchises. A single small store is not a way to get rich. But it may be a good first step--if you have a plan. The key to your plan must be a way of making your employees have value. Your stores must have busy employees. And your many stores must have many employees.

To get rich with a retail store, you need to develop a formula, a way of doing business. It must be simple so that others can follow it to the letter. Then you can open another store and use the same formula.

Your branch managers or franchisees can--and must--follow your formula.

MacDonald's has to be the most famous example of such a formula. Like MacDonald's, once you've got a formula that works, don't let your managers make changes by themselves. Make them pay a high price for their management job. Then they can't quit. Insist that they follow your orders. Plan and test every change, then enforce the change ruthlessly.

This can be done with any retail store. Set up a very specific product to sell. Arrange the store according to a fixed, simple plan. Advertise by tested methods. The formula is the thing. The formula can make you rich if more and more managers pay you for the right to follow your formula, and pay for the right to share their profits with you.

The secret is employees, but only working employees, not store clerks standing around, waiting for a customer.

Consider the history of an excellent retail-store location in my town. this location is at the entry to a shopping center. The people traffic is heavy past this location. But store after store failed there. The owners didn't know how.

One opened a gift shop. He had no employees. Day after day he sat at the cash register, doing nothing. I never saw a customer in the store. I never went in. One day I stood outside and analyzed why neither I nor anyone else would go in. The reason was obvious, everything in the store was visible from the outside. Why go in? Because no one went in, no one handled the gifts, and no one bought anything.

Perhaps a gift shop wasn't the right kind of store in that location. What followed was an ice-cream shop. With the many people going by and with no competition in the vicinity it looked like a sure thing. It lasted four months.

I went in one day to buy an ice-cream cone and find out why there were so few customers. After I worked my way through the crowd outside, I entered the almost vacant store, stood at the counter several minutes, listened to the waitresses talk to their boy- friends, got no ice-cream cone, and left. That was a month before it went out of business.

The owner of the ice-cream shop did not manage. He rented the space, set up the store, and withdrew. No one cared about the customers. There were employees, but they were not working. Employees are the Secret Source of wealth, but only if they are working.

*The next owner of the store at that location was my friends, the Wickards. They converted the ice-cream shop into a frozen-yogurt shop. The previous owner could have sold frozen yogurt very easily but he wasn't there.*

*The Wickard's shop is making a lot of money. They have now opened more stores. Their employees are working. What they are selling is good service by working employees. If their employees ever stop working, yogurt will go out of style--or so it may seem. The fact is, the product is not yogurt, it is service. Ice-cream, cookies, candy, vitamins, stationery; any number of different kinds of store could succeed in that location. But the employees would have to be working.*

---

1999 NOTE: I'm sorry to report that the Wickard's may have over-reached. The retail business is risky. A shopping mall where they had a store was not successful and pulled down its stores. The Wickards did very well otherwise. Smart people go on to other success.

# Action

1. Review your company organization, even if you have only one employee. Do you have workers or do you have overhead? Are there unnecessary managers? Right now, decide what to do about it. Act soon.

2. Plan how to let your employees make more of the decisions. Let them make some mistakes.

3. List your equipment, both owned and planned. Decide whether you should rent or buy. Consider possibilities of buying used equipment.

4. List your products. Evaluate each of them. What do they do for your customer? What really is the product?

5. Set aside your ego for a moment....are each of your products really good? Are you keeping one of them just because you've always claimed it's good and you don't want to admit you're wrong?

6. Do you need new or improved products to reduce your risk? Plan now on how to improve your product line.

7. Critically examine your products and your planned products for their relation to your present product line. Are they safely "in-line?" If not, study the differences. Can you make and sell them with your present ways of doing business? Decide now what to do about them.

8. Review your relation to the activities of your company. Are you in touch? Make a weekly plan of time to personally acquaint yourself with every activity in your business. (Don't meddle, just acquaint.)

9. Is there an indispensable person in your company? Are you he? Decide now on action to hire or train a back-up or replacement for any indispensable persons.

10. If you have a retail store, are your employees actually working full time? Put them to work. Have them rearrange the store. Have them make some product while waiting for customers to come in. Employees that aren't working will never make anyone rich.

11. Is there good reason for people to come into your store or contact your company? How many of the passing people come in? Is there a reason they should want to come in? How many of your potential customers and actual customers are you in touch with? Why so few? Make plans now to increase contact between your company and your customers.

# 11 – Million-Dollar Problems

You have the great advantage of understanding how the system works. Most millionaires did not know the system when they started their company. You know that employees produce wealth and that each employee is worth at least $40,000 to you. You also know about the positive feedback, called "bootstrapping," which will make your money grow. You know that you must advertise and that you must watch your cash supply.

But you may not know about some of the big problems. You will meet most of them in your business. You may not recognize them.

## The Problem with Problems

A typical list of business problems has such words as:

*"incompetence"*
*"unbalanced experience"*
*"lack of managerial experience"*
*"lack of experience in the line"*

Such lists tell us nothing. It is too easy to blame the manager for incompetence or inexperience. All first-time company founders are incompetent and inexperienced. All millionaires who didn't have rich fathers started both green and dumb.

What you need to know are the actual things that company founders do wrong. You need to know the specific things to be avoided.

Banks have an interest in the good management of the companies to which they make loans. Bank of America published a booklet called. Avoiding Management Pitfalls. They are a little more specific about the owner faults:

*1. Downgrading the need for experience*

*2. Sloppy record keeping*

*3. Reckless money management*

*4. Assuming an improper role*

*5. Failure to plan*

*6. Inattention to marketing*

*7. Ignoring the human factor*

What follows are comments on these owner faults, not necessarily in agreement with the bank. It is not the purpose of this book to scare you off by dwelling on pitfalls. Many millionaires have fallen into all the pits and dug themselves out, one by one. You can do it better because you are hereby forewarned.

## DOWNGRADING EXPERIENCE

No one has all the experience needed to found and manage a company. The need for experience is one reason for having employees. Besides doing the work, employees provide the knowledge you lack. If you lack a certain technical expertise, hire someone who has it and then stay out of his way. Rent a part-time consultant, join an industry association, talk to friendly competitors, customers, and suppliers.

If you know nothing about accounting, get a book-keeping service to keep your books. Hire a part-time accountant to go over the books and prepare your financial statements. The recording and management of money is where the lack of experience most often causes trouble for a new company owner.

SLOPPY RECORDS

RECKLESS MONEY MANAGEMENT


The new owner thinks he knows what's going on with his money and believes he doesn't need better records. The fact is, if he did know, he'd run the business differently.

Fortunately, the Internal Revenuers require some records to substantiate claims for tax deductions. Such deductions are hard to defend if the records are generally sloppy. It is because of the tax problem that most company owners have good records.

You should adopt a simple system of book-keeping from the start. Do not be sold a system too complex for the size and complexity of your company. A simple system will satisfy the tax collector and be easier for you to understand and use and keep correct.

Spend your money to advertise and produce your product, not for paper work. But do keep neat and complete records of all transactions. If necessary, later, an accountant can take that record and generate a detailed set of books.

Do have an accountant review your record-keeping occasionally to see how you are doing. He may be able to spot some leaks of your money which can be easily stopped. "Reckless money management" is usually the result of not knowing what your money is doing.

Company founders like you are pre-occupied with major problems and do not notice insidious errors which may be very costly. Correcting such errors may relieve the major problems. Common errors listed by Bank of America include: excessive inventory, border- line efforts on matters which cannot greatly benefit the company, purchase of excessive machinery which could have been rented, failure to take advantage of discounts, and failure to collect overdue customer's accounts.


*Don Ross bought a company which made a unique kind of furniture. After the customary problems one has in buying a company, such as lost process secrets, former owner walks out too soon, and unexpected bills, his company began to succeed. But the retail stores were slow to pay. The slow-paying stores kept ordering more furniture. They claimed they needed it so they could earn money to pay their bills. My inexperienced friend sent them more furniture. He should have sent a bill-collector first. Eventually my friend's company failed because it couldn't pay its own bills.*

Don't be anxious to sell to people who beg for shipments, but haven't yet paid for the previous shipments. Tell them you will ship as soon as they pay what they owe. They may reply, as one did, "Cancel the order. I can't wait that long."

---

1999 NOTE: I'm reminded of an incident that happened since I wrote this book. When one of our customer's was slow to pay, one of my salesmen went into their laboratory, put the machine on a cart and started out the door. This is not customary procedure and probably would be a violation of the Uniform Commercial Code. But it worked. The manager shouted, "hey, you can't do that" but arranged for the bill to be paid.

Whatever works.

---

## ASSUMING AN IMPROPER ROLE

"Wrong role" and "misuse of time" means that you, the owner, are spending time doing things you should hire someone to do. The founder (you) fiddles in the shop while Rome is burning in the marketing department. Most company founders are workers who know how to do things. They can do it better than anyone else--or think so. They ignore problems in other parts of the company while doing what they know how to do best, or feel most comfortable doing.

Doing what is most important means always dealing with problems. Problems are not comfortable. You must ask yourself each day, "What is the most important problem in my company?" Then you must work on that problem, no matter how it goes against your natural wish to have a happy day. Once you solve the number one problem, the satisfaction will pay you for the effort. You'll have a happy day.

You must hire people who help solve more problems than they create. Then you can take long vacations and spend some of your growing million dollars. By preparing your company to operate without you, you will make it more valuable to someone else. You can sell it for a million dollars. Make your company a salable package. but without wrapping yourself in it.

I have had many occasions to inspect small companies. The cause of impending failure is always evident in a few minutes of visiting and conversing with the company founder/manager.

There are many small companies which cannot be saved. What happens is that the founder builds a great fantasy of how his company is to be operated and how it must succeed. When failure can no longer be denied, a manager is brought in. The founder resists, in direct and in subtle ways, all attempts to change the operation of the company. He is mentally committed to his own ideas. He "knows" his ideas are good. To admit other-wise is more than his ego will permit. Because the owner maintains control--by knowledge of designs and processes, if not financially--the new manager is frustrated and leaves. Don't get into such a spot in either role.

## FAILURE TO PLAN

When you choose your product idea you must know what business you are going to be in. You must know who your customers are going to be, and what function your company is performing for them. Knowing that, you can plan the growth of your company.

You may think you are in the business of making and selling a particular product or line of products. In fact, you may be in the business of distributing products to a certain group of customers. In business textbooks, the Wrigley company is not regarded as a chewing-gum company. Instead, the Wrigley company is notable as a distributor. The innovation of the company was a distribution method for getting a low-priced product to many customers. They were so successful at this that they never needed to add more products to their line.

Many of the most successful companies grew because they recognized their real strength. The owner knew what business he was in, even if it wasn't the one he had originally planned. I have had close acquaintance with numerous new companies. It is remarkable how few were right in their original concept of their business.

*I was a manager in the research and development department of a company which was founded with a great deal of money. The intent was to manufacture a specific product as a base for the company. The company was never in its history able to manufacture that product. The reasons were highly technical and never understood. In spite of that, the company grew to gross sales of more than $20 million in a few years.*

*In the process of preparing to manufacture one product, the company had established the capability to manufacture others. After losing a few members of the founding group, the company discovered its product.*

You don't have to be right the first time. You must be ready to change your sights if you are missing the target. The stubborn founder deserves to lose who insists on staying with the original concept long after it has been proven wrong. Often, the successful business is much simpler than the original "great idea." The first idea is often too clever or too far ahead of its time.

One of the best sources of second ideas lies in the inability to produce the first idea. When for some reason, the first idea is failing, look closely at the reason. Perhaps the necessary material or machine is not available. Perhaps a new technique is needed. If you can supply what is missing, consider selling that as your product. Having found a solution, sell the problem.

*A company was set up in New Jersey to make sophisticated television test equipment. To work on this complex electronic apparatus, they needed a small laboratory tool--a controllable and precise power supply. They couldn't buy such things so they made their own. The resulting power-supply company was later sold for several million dollars. They were too busy getting rich to bother with the original idea.*

Your by-product may be the idea that will make you rich. Your by-product may also create a new problem. It may sell into a market that is new to you. For example, suppose you have started with a tool as your product, then learned a new process to make that tool. The process may be more valuable than the tool. But the process will sell to tool-makers, not to the tool- users who were your planned customers. You will have to pay attention to marketing.

## INATTENTION TO MARKETING

You know that you must advertise. But advertising is only one aspect of marketing. You must know who your customers are going to be. To reach them by advertising, you must know what they really want and what advertising they will see.

Many company founders are so proud of their product they assume that customers will come knocking on their door with cash in hand. Nothing is less true. Having identified your customers, you must determine what they really want, not just what you think they should want. Do they really want a product which has never existed--but which you can supply? Or do they want a cheaper version of the old, familiar product? Do they really want higher quality? Do they really want your product?

Once you know what they really want, how will you reach them? You must find a channel of communication and distribution. You must identify the customer and find out what he reads and from whom he buys. "You gotta know the territory."

*I know a man who didn't know the territory. He was induced by a company selling printing shops to rent a store location. It was one of those "non-franchise, franchise" deals which have appeared since laws were passed to regulate franchises. Such deals promise to do "market research" without specifying what they mean.*

*For this man the market research consisted of riding around town looking for a vacant store. Being trusting, although dismayed by the procedure, he rented the store, paid for the printing equipment and opened his shop. Then he began to learn about market research.*

*There were few customers in the territory. There was a lot of competition for those few.*

The market is the difference between the customers and the competition. If the supply already equals the demand, there is no market for you.

*The new print~shop owner soon learned about the supply in his territory. There was a print shop down the street one block. But that was the least of the competition.*

*His print shop had been located in a working-man's residential district. They were working. There were print shops hidden in the local garages. Independent printing salesman blanketed the territory, selling low-priced garage printing. The market, such as it was, was well served. He was in for a hard struggle to make a living.*

You must know the territory, the supply as well as the demand. The territory need not be geographic, as in the print-shop example. The territory can be a particular type of customer, scattered over the nation, perhaps small in number, but wanting your product. You may be able to reach them directly, through an existing distribution system, or by advertising in a specialty magazine. Montgomery Ward found such a territory.

When Montgomery Ward started his mail-order business, he identified a territory in need of his product: the farmers and their families. The farmers and their families were dependent on drummers. The drummers were traveling salesmen who went from farm to farm selling for a commission what they got from distributors who bought from manufacturers. Each "middle-man" raised the price so that the farmers were paying much more than the city people.

Montgomery bought from the manufacturer and sold directly to the farmer, without salesmen. He identified a special group of farmers who were prosperous and could be reached. He joined the Grange, a farm organization. As a member, he could use their mailing list. He mailed a one-page catalog. Four years later he mailed a 150 page catalog and was already a millionaire. He knew the territory--the Grange farmers.

If your product is derived from your personal experience, you will already know who the customers are.

If you are a baker and have a gadget to help bakers, you know where to find your customers. Send your sales brochure to bakeries, addressed to the "Chief Baker." If you have a better hole-maker for golf courses, find the golf courses in the phone books and send your sales literature to the "Head Greenskeeper."

You can get mailing lists for any specific group of customers. You can go and talk to the customers. You must do this to know the customers' reaction to your product.

Going and <u>listening</u> may well be the key to successful marketing. If your idea is new, your customers may not understand it. Then at least you know you have a problem. The most important marketing task then will be to educate your customers.

Education has limits. Too often, an inventor starts a company because he "knows" that people should use his product. He learns the hard way that it is only the customer's opinion that matters. The clever inventor has not only the usual problems of starting a company--he also has resistant customers. Do you need such a problem?

Start with a product the customers want immediately. Educate them later by offering your "great idea" as an alternative or as an additional product after you have established contact. The human factor with customers is similar to the human factors inside your plant.

## THE HUMAN FACTOR

Most small companies do not have serious people problems. A small company is usually a friendly place to work. The employees can see the business from door to door. They understand what the company is trying to do. They will pitch in and help when there is a problem. But all of this depends upon the owner. The owner, among other things, is a supervisor of people.

After many years of experience as a supervisor of many employees at many levels, from factory worker to department heads, I have no illusions about changing people. Neither this book, nor Dale Carnegie's, nor a management seminar will produce such changes. But there are some "tricks of the trade" you can learn to use.

Here are a few good ideas you should keep in mind:

*Listen to your employees.*

*Never criticize one before others.*

*Do praise one in front of others.*

*Make sure every one is busy.*

*Explain what you are trying to do.*

*Admit your own mistakes.*

New company founders usually listen to their employees. As your wealth increases and proves how smart you are, you may tend to stop listening. But as your company grows larger, it will be even more important to listen. You will be more isolated from the problems of the workers. Keep your ears open.

It's easy to jump on employees for errors you wouldn't make. By the same token, it's easy to take good work for granted and neglect to compliment the worker. The company owner must learn to be more sensitive than are most people. His position is unique among his workers.

Every employee must be busy at all times. Nothing is worse than a day with nothing to do. The effect on employee morale may be more costly than the direct loss of money caused by paid employees not producing. Have in mind some fill-in jobs to be done on quiet days.

You, as the owner of the company, usually know what you are trying to do. Your employees may not know.

Your employees will work more effectively if they do know the purpose of their work. Besides telling each employee the purpose of each task, you will do well to have regular meetings with all of your employees.

Bring your employees up to date on the state of the company business. Tell them the goals and how well they met the previous goals. Tell them how they will benefit if the company does well--and then make sure they do benefit.

Pay your employees the going wage or better. Make sure they feel they are getting fair pay for their work. Don't be a tight-wad with regard to your key and best employees. Pay them well. When your company is well on the way, give some thought to profit- sharing methods and provide generous fringe benefits to your long-term employees. As a small-company owner, you should have no union problems. When your company gets big you can incorporate and give your key long- term employees a little of the company. The next chapter tells of many things you can do when your company gets big.

In spite of this book and your best efforts, you will make some mistakes. You will ask employees to do things that don't work. You will try some products that fail. You will sometimes fail at your own tasks. These will help employee morale.

When you make a mistake, admit it freely and quickly. This will enable your employees to admit their errors and get on with the job. Some day, you and your employees can laugh all the way to the bank about the dumb mistakes you and they made, while you became a millionaire and they shared a little.

# Action

1. Identify the one area in which you are the weakest. Do you have an employee or an outside consultant helping you in that area? If not, take action to get help.

2. Review your book-keeping, have an accountant look at them. Keep your books simple, but make them complete. Are they giving you the information you need?

3. Tomorrow watch yourself at your company. Are you doing the important things a manager should be doing? Are you spending time on side matters that an employee could handle if you left him alone?

4. What are your plans for your company? Do you know what your product really is? Back off a moment and think about it. Why do people buy your product or service?

5. Make definite plans for a new product or service.

6. Take action to improve your marketing and plan how you can spend more time on marketing. Schedule visits with present and potential customers, if only a visit for your own information.

7. Decide who your customers are by class: doctors, carpenters, etc. Plan how to reach them.

8. Review your relations with your source of wealth: your employees. Plan now to compliment each of them once tomorrow. Make a list now.

# 12 – How You Can Make It Really Big

As a small-business owner, you should always be thinking of ways to make your business grow. If your business does not grow, it may shrink. Don't run that risk, make it big.

Healthy businesses, like people, are always growing--one way or another. Plan and have targets. Make targets of:

*1. new products,*

*2. increased sales,*

*3. more customers,*

*4. better trained employees,*

*5. faster accounting reports,*

*6. more help for you.*

Have fantasies of your giant company. All great things, and all little growing things, start with a fantasy. This is a fantasy chapter. You can make it come to life.

You should have in mind the eventual disposition of your company. You may want to run it until you retire at an old age. You may want to turn it over to your hired manager while you are still young. Or you may want to sell it quick, take your money, and go do some other thing. Start another company.

You can plan to live upstairs over your little shop or you can plan to own a lovely home and a vacation home and travel where you wish. It will be your choice.

It is no more difficult to create a large company which will make you wealthy than to manage a small company. In fact, the company growing large is a pleasure to manage. The small, wobbly company is a pain.

## Your Spiral of Expansion

Your first product is the seed for your company, but only the seed. It is the basis for starting, not the purpose and end of your company. The first product is the theme around which you arrange your employees: the source of your growing wealth. You may never make the product.

You can find someone to make the product for you, then your company will advertise it, sell it, distribute it, and make enough money to expand. Perhaps you can then make the product. Or make a part of it. Or assemble it from parts you buy.

Perhaps you are making a product but having someone else distribute it. You can expand your company by doing your own distribution. What you are looking for is an excuse to have more employees. They are worth $40,000 each to you and they don't cost half that much. Get more of them.

Perhaps you have one salesman contacting retailers or distributors. Could he do some of the distribution if he had an assistant? Perhaps, instead of using manufacturer's representatives, you should build a sales department that can represent you. You can start with your local area and work outward. As your sales grow you will eventually have a complete distribution system and a lot of employees. But one product is not enough. If it fails, your company will die.

## THE SPIRAL PATHS OF YOUR COMPANY'S GROWTH

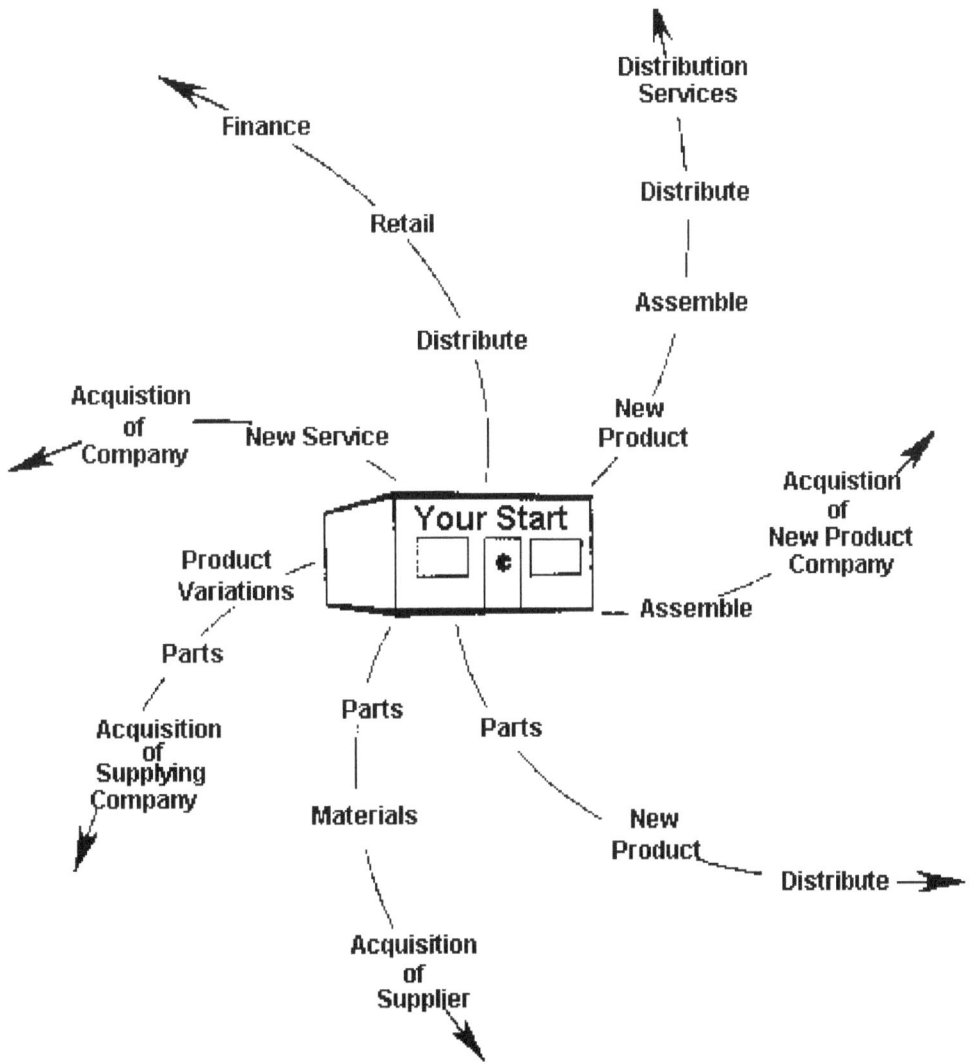

Look for new products. As you get more employees, especially salesmen, your employees will recommend new products.

In addition to new products you can expand and diversify your company around any product by making a vertical company.

## VERTICAL INTEGRATION

When you expand your company by doing more of the things necessary to convert raw materials into a product in the users hands, you are expanding vertically. Adding new products is called horizontal expansion.

For example, an oil company is vertical if it drills for oil, pumps it out of the ground, pipelines it to a refinery, refines it, trucks it to a gas station owned by the oil company, and sells it to the final consumer. You can do the same.

Your product will require some parts or material. Your retail store will need things to sell. You can expand by making some of your own parts of products. This will keep your employees busy.

The grocer who owns some land out of town and grows some of the vegetables he sells is vertically integrated. But don't get carried away.

The founder of the Chun King Chinese-food company, Jeno Paulucci, tells of the mistake he made by trying to grow his own celery. Growing celery is an agricultural art. His company didn't have the art. He had to get out of the celery business.

Stay out of the celery business. Any business you don't understand will be a celery business for you. Do what you know how to do.

When you start, you will depend upon suppliers. Some of these suppliers will be doing simple things that you can do. Some of the suppliers will be doing things badly. You can do better. You know what your suppliers customers want--you are one.

Make it a cardinal rule never to be at the mercy of suppliers. Have more than one supplier for everything you need. If you cannot find two reliable suppliers, you have found a need. Become a supplier for that article.

Look for customers for your new capability, but don't help your competition. You have now begun to integrate horizontally. You have a new kind of product.

## HORIZONTAL INTEGRATION

When you add a new product or service you are expanding horizontally. The new product may be related to your first product. It may be a part or an assembly of that product. Or the new product may be unrelated and you may be in trouble.

You must recognize the differences that are important. The "rules of the game" may not be the same. You may have to deal with a different set of customers with quite different manners and practices.

*Hewlett-Packard found that it could not depend on its suppliers for certain critical parts for its products. It set up a new division to make these critical parts.*

*I was a manager in that division. The division was successful. It produced the critical parts and sold them to outside customers at a profit. But there was a chronic problem.*

*The parts were not sold to the regular customers of the large company. The big corporation sales department did not understand the product.*

*The selling methods differed. The manner of pricing the product was not the same. The parent company sold its catalog of products at fixed prices. The customers of the parts division wanted custom specifications for each part and a negotiated price. The parent company sold its products one at a time. The components company needed to sell by the thousands.*

*The large company wanted to sell all its products, including the parts, through one marketing department and with one crew of salesmen. It seemed more efficient but didn't work.*

*Because of the failure to understand that the new products were different in important ways, the organization of the new division was subject to frequent changes. The parent company could not resist trying to make its child conform.*

> 1999 NOTE: In spite of its non-conformity, the small components company is now a billion-dollar company. With persistence the problems can be solved. Children do eventually grow up and leave home.

If you get into such a situation, hire experts and let them do their thing. You don't know everything just because you are a millionaire. Many owners of successful businesses make the mistake of believing they are great geniuses. The fact is that it doesn't take genius to become a millionaire in the U.S.

Horizontally or vertically, every skill in your company and every facility you control can expand. Look at what your company can do. Sell that ability. Sell the service.

Do accounting for another small company. Do packaging for some new entrepreneur. Offer to sell his product through your distribution system. Rent used space to a new company on a short-term lease. If you have a machine that is only used part time, offer it as a service. Put an evening shift on such machines. Make the machines pay for themselves.

Look particularly for experts among your employees. Build a new company around such an expert. He'll be happy. You'll get rich faster.

Your object is to assemble a jigsaw puzzle. The pieces must fit to one another. Don't build a haystack full of needles. You'll get stuck.

*One company I knew let things get out of hand. The owner thought that expansion meant adding anything. He added everything he could get his hands on. But nothing fitted.*

*His plant became a clutter of odds and ends of little companies. Scraps of unused equipment and unused people filled the building. A new manager was imposed on the founder. The new manager had trucks carting the odds and ends to the junkyard every day for three months. The company never did recover from the unenlightened expansion and belated contraction.*

1999 NOTE: The company was sold. The new owner, an east-coast company, struggled manfully for a year or two, then gave up--finding itself unable to manage from a distance--and sold it to a west-coast company. The building is now gone. By an odd coincidence, the original owner--a fine gentleman-- was later my stockbroker. You must have some plan for each and every expansion you make. The new activity must fit. The sum of the old and the new pieces must be more valuable than either by itself.

## THE VALUE OF GOOD GROOMING

You, the company owner, will have possibilities without limit. But there are some fundamentals which you should attend to from the start even in the planning of a new company.

To sell a company or to borrow money or to sell shares, your company must be *well-groomed*.

Let me tell you about a company that was not well-groomed, and the consequences for the owners.

*I was a member of a committee of three managers who evaluated a small company. The company was very new and very small. In fact, there were only the three founders. They had certain skills. Their product would have mated well with the products of the company I represented. But the company was not well-groomed.*

*They had rented adequate space in which to manufacture their product. Had we acquired them, we would have moved them into our existing large plant. So you might think the appearance of their plant would not have been important. In fact, it was decisive. We did not acquire them.*

*They had failed to prepare a plan. They talked of how they would manufacture their product. But nowhere on paper, or with chalk lines on the floor, was there a display of a plan. I could envision a layout of the manufacturing area--an arrangement of machines and assembler ladies and test stations and a shipping area.*

*The three company owners may have had such a vision. They didn't show it. If they had taken one hour to move a few benches into place and to mark locations with chalk on the floor--if they had groomed the place-they would have received financing and would probably be wealthy now.*

Grooming counts. Good grooming shows the world that you know what you are doing. And what you plan to do.

Usually the most important grooming is the preparation of the accounting records. Not just the financial statements--auditors for the buyers look at other books: customer lists, inventory records, advertising responses, employee records, your personal income tax reports, etc.

Orderly books impress the bankers much more than does a good product. They don't understand how a small company operates. They don't understand much of anything except the money books. That is their business. Unfortunately, the money books really don't tell whether a company is a success or not. But that's beside the point.

If a banker visits you, you must show good accounting records. If a stockholder visits you, you must show him how fast "his" company is growing. If a customer visits you, you must have piles of products to show him you can deliver. If a supplier visits you, you must show him how much you are growing and how much you will buy from him in the future if he is a good supplier.

Good grooming starts before your company begins. Your planning should include the factors which make for a good-looking company. Begin with your choice of product.

Is the product one that will look good to a banker? You know it must look good to the customer, but the bankers and future investors or the some day buyer of your company have a different point of view. You may want some money from them. You may want to sell out for your $1,000,000.

Bankers and investors can most easily be impressed by a product they do not understand. Some kind of magic scientific machine can always be financed. A product that cannot even be seen is also impressive. A gold mine in Texas or a product too secret to be shown will always find bankers.

Bankers and investors best understand money. They little understand real things. That is why mysterious machines are easy to finance. If you want to go the big financing route, find a scientific product. Make your product impressive.

After the product, consider the package. The Pet Rock was not much of a product but the package was great. Many products, including some breakfast cereals, don't amount to much. But the package is great.

Right from the start, look at your company from all points of view. Is it well-groomed? Does it look like a good, growing, profitable company or does it look disorganized, unplanned, unsure of its own identity?

How your company looks may very well decide its fate at the hands of your bankers, customers, suppliers, and your employees.

Your employees will work harder and more effectively if they feel they are a part of a good-looking company. Well-ordered work space, well-planned work, reasonable but tough quotas of expected production, and businesslike managers will get more output from your employees. The Secret Source will produce more wealth for you.

The name you choose is a part of its grooming. Don't be frivolous when you choose a name. And don't be in a hurry to add "Inc."

## DON'T INCORPORATE

Don't incorporate unless you have a definite reason for doing so. You cannot escape responsibility for your debts by making your small, one-owner business a corporation. No bank will loan money to such a corporation without getting a claim on the assets of the owner. In any case, the little company already holds most of your personal assets. If you incorporate it and borrow too much money you could lose your shirt.

There are three valid reasons for incorporation. The first is the reason for the existence of corporations: being free from liability. The corporation's debt are not your debts. The second is the income tax. When your income tax can be reduced by reporting your company separately--only possible if it's a corporation--then you should make that change. Corporations have many tax advantages.

The third reason for incorporating your company is to share the ownership. You may want to do this as a way of raising money or to give your employees a piece of the action. Then your Secret Source of wealth will make you richer quicker.

Money raised by selling shares of your company need never be repaid. The share holder hopes your company will grow and increase in value so that the stock market will raise the value of his or her shares. Dividends, if there are any, may help raise the market value of the stock.

Because the money need never be repaid, and almost never is repaid, the capital it provides gives your company a "pad" against hard times. This can be seen in those large corporations that have raised money by selling stock, paying little or no dividends, and borrowing little. They couldn't go into bankruptcy if they wanted to. In any emergency they have the ability to borrow enough to carry them over until better times.

Shares in the company are one of the best employee incentives. A Christmas bonus or profit-sharing bonus is a one-time thing. Owning a share of the company gives your employees a continuing interest in the success of your company.

When you have a corporation you will have much additional paper work. A separate income tax form must be filed. You must collect additional information for the IRS. You must report to the corporation commissioners, state tax agents, security commissions, shareholders and others. You must pay more for lawyers and accountants. But you can get some of it back.

It will be easier to avoid income taxes. Many tax-avoidance gimmicks will be available to you. The lawyer and accountant you must have can earn their pay by cutting your taxes. Be certain they are aggressive tax-cutters.

The courts have made it clear that you do not need to pay any taxes you can legally avoid. Keep your money. Some day incorporation will help.

No doubt you have heard about the advantages of incorporating in Delaware. You've heard of a book called *How to Form Your Own Corporation Without a Lawyer for Under $50*. The book tells you how to incorporate in Delaware by mail order. It can be done. Hewlett-Packard changed its incorporation from California to Delaware for their own good reasons. But they did so after they were well established.

You can get into a really complicated tangle if you incorporate in a "foreign" state and then try to sell stock in your home state. By the time you get through, you may pay a lawyer much more than if you'd hired a lawyer in the first place.

This is not to say there are no advantages in incorporating in certain states such as Delaware of Nevada. There are. These states have corporation laws designed for the benefit of corporation managers. They make a profitable business of selling charters to those managers.

Nevada sells corporate charters to California companies. The companies establish an office in Nevada or perhaps a small facility with one or two employees. They open a bank account in Nevada. If there are only one or two owners, they may establish residency in Nevada on one day of the year, they avoid California property tax on their inventory.

---

1999 NOTE: California had to change its tax on company assets because the roads were clogged by trucks moving assets to Nevada on the counting day. It is common for a company to incorporate in its home state, then change to a better state when the company gets large. The managers choose a state that gives them the greatest personal advantages, especially the right to do as they please with the company.

Delaware, the state of the Du Ponts, has long been the favorite.

---

When your time is right, incorporation will make it possible to sell shares to raise money to grow faster. You can give shares to your key employees, or to all of them, so as to motivate them and keep them. You can avoid taxes more easily. You can borrow money without risking your personal assets. You can print shares of stock and use this self-printed money to buy other companies. You can pump up the price of the shares and sell out for a good price--better than you could get as sole proprietor. All these goodies in good time.

HOW TO SELL OUT FOR MILLIONS--
AND KEEP YOUR COMPANY

You can sell your company and still keep control of it. What you will do is to incorporate, sell shares, then when the shares are widely distributed, you can sell your own shares. Keep some, say 5% of the total.

Sell your shares when you know the price is. high. You'll have your first million or two, but you can get more.

After you incorporate, choose a board of directors. The members of the board should be mostly your employees. You can fire them if they don't always vote your way on the board.

Get a retired big wheel from a giant corporation on your board. His biography will impress the bankers and the shareholders. He'll enjoy the board meetings with the deluxe dinner at a private club. He will cause you no trouble by thinking.

Your bank or other source of money will probably want a representative on your board of directors. He will be ignorant about your company and will follow your lead. Keep close to him, though, his ignorance can cause trouble. With this board of your own choosing, you can retain complete control of your company.

To protect yourself even more, you should arrange any loans or lines of credit to contain a clause to the effect that if the present management is removed, the loans will come due: and the lines of credit will be cancelled. The bank will be willing to add this clause for its own protection against a takeover vulture corporation seeking to use your company's assets.

Now you've got your money and the company too. That is not the end of your possibilities. Some day the price of the shares of your company will go down. The stock market does wondrous things. Even if you have a steady profit, the stock may fall to a fraction of its usual price. When this happens you can help matters by reporting a lower profit.

Profit can always be shifted from one quarter to the next and can be decreased in any one quarter by extra buying and by postponing sales. In addition, you can use the moment to write off any inventory that has questionable value. The net effect will be delightful. The value of your company will fall.

When your company's stock is priced low, you can use the company's cash and borrowing ability to buy the stock. Corporations often buy their own stock from their shareholders.

With luck, you can buy most of the stock. But don't sell your own personal shares. Then your share of the company will increase. Shares owned by the company do not vote for the board of directors. You will become the majority shareholder. This is called "going private." You again become the sole owner of the company.

There may be a few shareholders who hold out. You can scare them into selling their shares by making a "final" offer. Warn them that they may never again be able to sell their stock.

You have held onto your own stock, perhaps five percent of the whole. But you are the only stockholder. You own the company. You can sell it. You can "spin off" pieces for cash. You'll have a staff of lawyers to help you do things legally, if perhaps a little too aggressively.

This is no fantasy. It has been done. Keep control of your company. One more factor will be valuable if someday you decide to sell your company. That factor is serendipity. When two plus two equals seven, that is serendipity. It means that your company plus another company will be worth more than the sum of the two standing apart. A lucky combination of products may have this profitable result. What you need is a good mate for your company.

## MATE AND GET RICH QUICKER

Suppose, for example, that your company makes a new CB (citizen's band antenna for mounting on autos. Such a product, and the employees who can make it, may be very valuable to a company that manufactures CB equipment or sells such equipment but doesn't have its own antenna to sell.

*When my friend and former business associate, Bernie Mills, sold his company, the buying company (a giant corporation) quickly dropped his product. What they kept was his group of employees. The employees were what they wanted and what they paid for. My friend retired at 43.*

It is not unusual for an acquired company to be dismantled and only the employees kept. The employees are the "thing of value" that has changed hands. Sometimes the acquiring company does not understand this and causes such confusion that the key employees all jump to other jobs, leaving an empty shell' of little value. Keep this danger in mind when you buy another company.

To live like a millionaire, you need to build your company up to at least seven, and possibly as many as fourteen employees. In retail you need more. To sell your company for $1,000,000 you may need twenty-five employees and a good prospect for growth. At $40,000 each, 25 employees should bring a million dollars for you easily.

## AND WHEN YOU ARE RICH

By now, you've started to apply some of the things you've learned. You can see how your company can grow.

What will you do once you are a millionaire? You have read the good news, now here's some bad news. After you are rich and own a growing company, you will not want to stop.

You will be free to quit if you wish, but you won't. Keeping your company growing will be too much fun. Only employees retire. They retire because they don't really like what they are doing. A company owner like you doesn't need to retire. You are doing all the things you want to do. Why quit? By hiring managers--more of the secret source; employees--you can sit back, travel, vacation, do what you please, while your managers run the business. But stay in touch.

As your company grows you must change your role. You must let go. You must let your employees make decisions, even though they will make mistakes--some you would not have made--and some you would have made. Can you stand to let someone else make the mistakes?

Many companies operate for many years at the one-million dollar level with an owner who cannot let the company get any larger--or doesn't chose to. Such a company may generate a millionaire's income, but not be saleable because of the indispensability of the owner.

Many companies get into trouble at a critical level which depends upon the nature of the business. For your kind of company that level is at total sales of $20,000,000. At that size the manager may lose intimate contact with the operation. His control becomes weak because he can no longer make the essential decisions.

If a good management crew has not been hired and trained, the company may run in the wind like a ship with no helmsman. Companies of this size often undergo reorganizations. The owner, manager, or board of directors struggle to find a combination that can run the drifting company.

You may be wise to sell out before your company reaches the $20,000,000 sales level.

As the owner of a company who knows the American millionaire's Secret Source of wealth, you may get too rich. As that time approaches, you may want to use stocks options and a stock-purchase plan to share your company with your employees. Sharing your wealth with your Secret Source may be the ultimate way to get still richer.

# Action

Use the principles you have learned in this book and:

1. Make plans for the future of your company.

    a. List the possible paths of expansion:

    b. Make a schedule for your study of what needs to be done to get started on those paths.

    c. Immediately find out about one way to expand, and take action to start that expansion.

2. Inspect the grooming of your company and take action to improve it.

    a. Is your product or service one that is appealing to investors?

    b. Does your work space look like a well-organized business?

    c. Are your money books in good order? Are they complete?

    d. Do you have an advertising program that has been tested?

    e. Do you have skilled employees who make a good impression on your customers?

    f. Do you have plans on paper to show investors how your company will grow? (You need these plans even if you never sell your company.) OR are you growing by re-investing profits and need to investors?

    g. OR your choice: be happy with your company as it is, and.....

# Congratulations!

## You have graduated.  Here is your certificate:

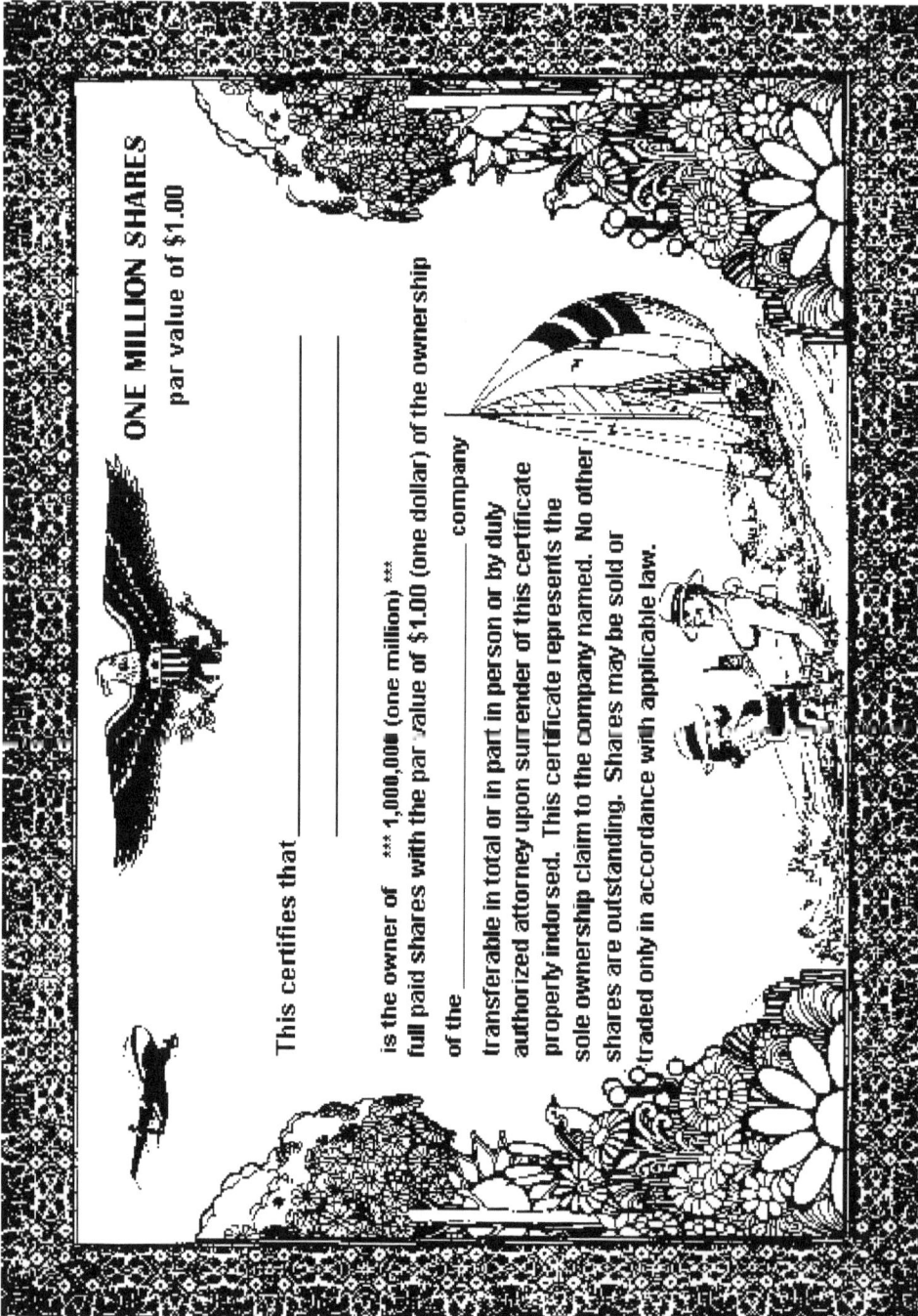

**ONE MILLION SHARES**
par value of $1.00

This certifies that
_____

is the owner of   *** 1,000,000 (one million) ***
full paid shares with the par value of  $1.00 (one dollar) of the ownership
of the _____ company

transferable in total or in part in person or by duly
authorized attorney upon surrender of this certificate
properly indorsed.  This certificate represents the
sole ownership claim to the company named.  No other
shares are outstanding.  Shares may be sold or
traded only in accordance with applicable law.

www.ingramcontent.com/pod-product-compliance
Lightning Source LLC
Chambersburg PA
CBHW061617210326
41520CB00041B/7479